The Medieval Castle

Other titles in the *History's Great Structures* series include:

The Eiffel Tower
The Great Wall of China
The Parthenon of Ancient Greece
The Roman Colosseum
Shakespeare's Globe Theater
The World Trade Center

History's Great
STRUCTURES

The Medieval Castle

Stephen Currie

ReferencePoint Press®

San Diego, CA

© 2014 ReferencePoint Press, Inc.
Printed in the United States

For more information, contact:
ReferencePoint Press, Inc.
PO Box 27779
San Diego, CA 92198
www.ReferencePointPress.com

LIBRARY OF CONGRESS CATALOGING-IN-PUBLICATION DATA

Currie, Stephen, 1960-
 The medieval castle : part of the History's great structures series / by Stephen Currie.
  pages cm. -- (History's great structures)
 Includes bibliographical references.
 ISBN 978-1-60152-536-9 (hardback) -- ISBN 1-60152-536-2 (hardback) 1. Castles--Juvenile
literature. 2. Castles--Design and construction--Juvenile literature. 3. Architecture, Medieval--
Juvenile literature. 4. Civilization, Medieval--Juvenile literature. I. Title.
 NA7710.C87 2014
 728.8'10902--dc23
                                                                          2013009271

CONTENTS

IMPORTANT EVENTS IN THE HISTORY OF MEDIEVAL CASTLES

476
Fall of the Roman Empire.

CA. 1078
Work begins on the Tower of London.

CA. 800
Motte and bailey becomes a popular type of castle.

1066
William the Conqueror is crowned king of England.

CA. 1170
Work on the Krak des Chevaliers is completed.

600   800   1000   1200

CA. 1000
Stone keeps begin to appear.

CA. 750
Vikings begin raids on Europe.

CA. 1200
Concentric castles become common in Europe.

CA. 1100
Stone becomes increasingly common in castle walls.

CA. 1230
Birth of castle designer Master James of St. George.

1838
Renovation of Wartburg Castle in Germany begins.

1295
Work begins on Beaumaris Castle, the last of Edward I's castles in Wales.

CA. 1350
End of the medieval period and the beginning of the Renaissance.

CA. 1450
Guns become the most effective siege weapons.

1300   **1500**   **1700**   **1900**

CA. 1500
The era of castle construction comes to an end.

2006
Krak des Chevaliers is named a UNESCO World Heritage Site.

1304
Edward I captures Stirling Castle by means of the trebuchet Warwolf.

1820
Sir Walter Scott's nostalgic medieval novel *Ivanhoe* is published.

CA. 1275
Gunpowder is introduced into Europe.

The Castle

For most people today the term *castle* calls to mind an enormous stone structure on the top of a hill. In the popular imagination, castles feature thick walls forming a nearly impenetrable barrier to attack, towers rising high above the walls, and a water-filled moat with a wooden drawbridge. There might also be cold, cramped prison cells or long, stone staircases that spiral up to the tops of the towers. Moreover, the stereotypical castle includes sumptuous suites for the noble family who lived there. And most people would agree that a castle has a particular atmosphere, an overall mood, which—depending on the castle, its setting, and its inhabitants—can vary from forbidding to romantic.

These images of castles come in part from popular culture. Many Walt Disney animated features, notably *Cinderella*, *Snow White*, and *Sleeping Beauty*, take place in and around castles. Live-action movies, such as *Dracula* and *Monty Python and the Holy Grail*, highlight castles prominently as well. So do books (and the movies made from them), such as those in the *Harry Potter* series. Castles are common themes in video games, too. In the *Castlevania* series of games, for instance, players need to force their way into a castle belonging to the legendary Count Dracula. The *Stronghold* series allows players to build castles and defend them in addition to attacking enemy fortifications, and the *Thief* series, in contrast, challenges players to find hidden treasure inside a castle's mazelike passageways.

The people who make movies, write novels, and design video games invent castles that best suit their own purposes. Indeed, some of these fictional castles are not even architecturally possible—particularly because many, like Hogwarts in the *Harry Potter* novels, are set in a world of magic. Even so, the castles described in these works are based at least loosely on historical fact. During the medieval period, or Middle Ages, an era that lasted from about 500 to approximately 1350, castles were a common sight across Europe and parts of the Middle East. Many of these castles, especially the largest ones, inspired the fictional castles of modern times. The castle in the Disney film *Cinderella*, for example, draws some of its features from the Spanish medieval castle Alcázar of Segovia, along with several others.

The fictional castles of modern times are imposing and evocative. But then, so were the actual castles of the medieval period. The largest of these were enormous structures, every bit as large and awe-inspiring as the castles of animated film and video gaming. Malbork Castle in what is now Poland, for example, sprawls across 5 square miles (13 square km); Warwick Castle in Great Britain rises 128 feet (39 m) above the ground. The smaller castles of the Middle Ages were impressive achievements, too. In an era long before power tools, standard measurement systems, and mass production, the medieval period produced castles that were sturdy, well-designed, and solidly built. Indeed, the greatest of them are widely accepted as among the most remarkable and beautiful examples of architecture anywhere on the globe.

Building a Castle

The credit for the castles of the Middle Ages goes to a variety of people. The lords who bankrolled construction of these structures typically joined forces with architects and master craftsmen to develop plans for their fortification. Ordinary laborers, most of them peasants—the largest social class in the medieval world—dug foundations, carted timber, and lifted stones into place. Skilled woodworkers and stonecutters took care of the finer details, such as carving rocks into final shape, determining where to place beams

Nestled in the hills above the Moselle River in Germany, the formidable medieval Burg Eltz Castle once provided homes for three large families. Within its walls were eighty rooms, forty fireplaces, and a chapel.

to maximize the castle's strength, or adding the small architectural flourishes that distinguished castles from Ireland to Syria. The construction of castles, then, was a group effort involving hundreds upon hundreds of laborers drawn from all walks of life.

The castles of the Middle Ages that survive today are noted, and rightly so, for the care that went into their construction, the complexity of their design, and their stark beauty. But these features were merely by-products of the castle's two main purposes. One of these was to provide living quarters for the monarchs or nobles who owned the structures. Indeed, most definitions of a castle require it to be occupied by people other than soldiers. To this end, castles typically included rooms that could be used by lords and ladies for eating, sleeping, and entertaining guests. Though these suites were seldom as comfortable or luxurious as those belonging to movie castles, they were well-appointed by the standards of the medieval era. That was especially true of castles built in the later years of the period.

The most important reason to build a castle, however, did not involve comfort. Rather, it was military necessity. A sturdy castle presented a barrier to attackers, making it problematic or virtually impossible for an army to make its way inside the structure's walls. Thus, the castle's primary purpose was to offer protection in wartime for soldiers, nobles, and peasants. In this way a castle was like an inhabited fort—only, in most cases, larger and more

difficult to conquer. The walls, the towers, the moats, the narrow windows in the stonework, the trapdoors in the floors—all were in place to make castles stronger and more impervious to attack.

The world of fictional castles is an intriguing one, mixing as it does historical fact with modern imagination. But the reality of medieval castles is even more fascinating than the make-believe castles of imagination. Though the castles of the Middle Ages lack vampires and sorcery, the details of their construction, use, and development are nonetheless compelling. From the stone carvers who painstakingly shaped rock for castle walls to the attacking soldiers who tunneled underneath the castle's towers, from the deliberately fouled moats surrounding medieval fortresses to modern efforts to preserve the structures that still survive, the castles of the Middle Ages tell a dramatic story of hard work, resourcefulness, and seemingly endless warfare. They remain today a testament to the power, creativity, and determination of the people who designed, built, and defended them.

CHAPTER ONE

Beginnings and Influences

The Middle Ages were sandwiched between two generally prosperous periods of European history: the Roman Empire and the Renaissance. The Roman Empire, headquartered in the Italian city of Rome, flourished for many centuries before collapsing in the late 400s. The Renaissance, deeply influenced by the Romans' ideas and achievements, began in about 1350 and lasted about two hundred years. Each era is well known today for its cultural achievements, its political innovations, and its emphasis on commerce. In contrast to the pioneering periods that surrounded it, the medieval era has long been considered dull and unoriginal. And indeed, in many ways the European Middle Ages were quite static, with relatively few changes from one decade—or century—to the next.

In one aspect of life, however, the medieval period was very nearly as productive

WORDS IN CONTEXT
static
Unchanging.

as the eras around it. That aspect was technology. The Roman Empire and the Renaissance are known for impressive technological achievements—Rome was noted for its network of roads, for example, and the printing press was developed during the Renaissance—but the medieval period developed dozens of useful technologies as well. As historian Elspeth Whitney writes, "The sheer number and variety of technological innovations in the Middle Ages is noteworthy."[1] These innovations included waterpower and mechanical clocks along with improvements in looms, agricultural tools, and weaponry.

The medieval emphasis on technology is most obvious, however, in engineering and architecture. Some of the most remarkable buildings ever created date from the medieval period. These include cathedrals—enormous churches dedicated to the glory of the Christian God—and perhaps even more notably, castles. Constructed to be both defensive bulwarks and homes for the very rich, medieval castles represented something fundamentally new in European history. The castles of the Middle Ages, however, were not only innovative; they were sturdy, well built, and a strategic response to the political and military conditions prevailing at the time. As historians Frances Gies and Joseph Gies put it, the largest and best-designed medieval castles represent "the engineering marvels of the age."[2]

Forts of the Romans

At the beginning of the medieval period—about AD 500—Europe had no castles, at least not as the term is understood today. At the end of the period, roughly 850 years later, castles were a common sight across much of the European continent and into the Middle East. It is not possible, though, to identify a particular year or decade as the point at which castle construction began. Even singling out a specific century is difficult. Though many historians cite the 800s as the time when castle construction became popular, that view is not universal. Castle design and construction evolved in fits and starts as the medieval period went on, with each age adding new ideas and modifying existing designs. Rather than being credited to just one part of the Middle Ages, then, the castle was the collective invention of many generations of medieval builders, craftsmen, and engineers.

Although castles were clearly a creation of the Middle Ages, some aspects of castle design and construction techniques date from long before the start of the medieval era. During the heyday of the Roman

RECYCLED FORTIFICATIONS

The motte and bailey castles of the 800s and 900s were sometimes built from scratch. Kings or other nobles might see a need for a castle in a particular spot and order one to be constructed there. However, the lords of the Middle Ages saw little reason to build entirely new castles when Roman fortifications still existed—and in the prime years of motte and bailey construction, many Roman forts still survived. When they could, then, nobles of the medieval period made use of these fortifications as a base for their newer designs.

In some cases, this meant recycling the materials the Romans had used to build something in the same place. In others, especially when the original forts were better preserved, it meant strengthening the existing walls and adding living quarters on the inside of the structure. Portchester Castle in England and Colwyn Castle in Wales are two examples of motte and baileys known to have incorporated earlier Roman fortifications into their designs.

In turn, the motte and baileys that were common before 1100 were often recycled themselves in later years as castle designs changed. Again, lords rarely saw the sense in building something entirely new when there was an existing fortification that could be made stronger. Portchester Castle, which had originally been a Roman fort, is among many European motte and baileys strengthened by the addition of stone walls and other updated features. In this way, the history of the medieval castle is one of constant refurbishing and redesign.

Empire, Roman soldiers constructed a variety of forts across Europe. Most of these forts were built to house soldiers and to fend off attacks from enemies, of which there were many—quite a few Europeans, especially those to the north of Rome, did not appreciate Roman rule. The walls of these forts provided a barrier to invaders, and Roman soldiers out to conquer new territory or put down rebellions could use the fortifications as a base for these activities. Remains of Roman forts can still be found in many European countries.

The Roman fortresses were almost never used as homes for nobles and other leaders, so historians rarely consider them castles in the medieval sense. The Roman forts did nonetheless resemble the castles of the Middle Ages in some important ways. Like medieval castles, for example, Roman fortifications had walls made of wood or stone, and the largest Roman forts were as spacious as the castles of later Europe—archaeological evidence suggests that some Roman forts could hold a garrison of one thousand soldiers. And there is a connection between the Latin and English words used to describe forts of the Roman Empire and castles of medieval Europe. The Latin names for a Roman fortification were *castrum* or *castellum*; over time, these became the modern English word *castle*.

As the Roman Empire waned in power and influence, Roman forces gradually retreated toward Rome or were pushed in that direction by other Europeans. Many Roman fortresses remained, however. Recognizing the military value of these structures, the new rulers of Europe made at least some use of the forts. In 500, for example, soldiers from two warring groups, the Burgundians and the Franks, fought one another in what is now southern France. At one point during the conflict, Burgundian soldiers occupied an early Roman fortification. Though Clovis, the king of the Franks, tried to push the Burgundians out of the fort, he was unsuccessful. In the words of one of Clovis's advisers, "The stronghold is too well fortified for you to capture."[3]

In addition to using Roman fortifications, the people of the early Middle Ages—roughly, the years between 500 and 800—also built some forts of their own. Construction on Silves Castle in Portugal, for example, is known to have begun in the 700s, and archeological evidence suggests that several other European castles date from this period as well. Early medieval peoples also spent time repairing and strengthening existing Roman fortifications. In some cases they made important changes to the fort's original design. At one Romanian site, notes historian Peter Purton, early medieval builders added a tower to an existing fortification. And a former Roman fort in the

Silves Castle in Portugal (pictured) is an example of an early medieval fortress. Construction began on the structure sometime in the 700s and when it was complete, it probably formed part of the walls surrounding the town of the same name.

Alps was reinforced by the addition of a new wall at some point in the late 500s.

Changes in War

In general, however, fortifications were not enormously important in the early Middle Ages. The historical and archeological record suggests that relatively few forts were built during this time. And the number of refurbished Roman fortresses was dwarfed by the number that went to ruin following the collapse of the empire. In part, the de-emphasis on forts was the result of the style of warfare most common at the time. Since weapons of the early Middle Ages were usually designed to be used in close combat, battles were most often fought in open fields where soldiers could hack at one another with swords, impale their enemies with spears and lances, and take aim at their opponents with bows and arrows. Under these circumstances, a fortification, no matter how sturdy, was not especially helpful.

Nor did the political and economic situation of the time support an emphasis on castles. With the end of the Roman Empire, Europe's wealth began to dwindle. Between the years 500 and 800, royal treasuries were largely empty. With no pressing military need to build imposing castles, it was difficult for kings to justify spending their limited funds on massive forts. Moreover, the collapse of Rome had resulted in a patchwork of hundreds of small political units all across Europe, creating a situation in which few rulers had the ability to raise a massive army. Indeed, armies of the early Middle Ages rarely had more than 150 soldiers. "Political division, strategic situations, and financial predicaments probably did not justify the maintenance or creation of new strongholds,"[4] sums up historian Jean-Denis Lepage.

The lack of emphasis on castle construction does not imply that warfare was uncommon in the early medieval years. On the contrary, warfare was frequent throughout this period and was in fact very nearly routine. European leaders of the period were generally uninterested in seeking diplomatic solutions to disputes. Instead, their automatic response to insult, oppression, and overlapping land claims was to attack. Fighting swirled across Germany, the Balkans, Spain, and England, as kings, popes, and princes launched full-scale attacks on their enemies, assisted by an ever-changing assortment of allies. "There were wars between protagonists at every level," writes historian Maurice Keen. "The resort to violence was a ready one in the middle ages, at every level of authority."[5]

But although warfare was nearly constant in medieval times, political conditions and military strategies were not. Beginning around the year 800, two important changes took place in Europe, both of which pushed military strategists toward a greater appreciation of forts. The first of these was an increase in raids by well-armed and powerful outsiders. Most notable among these, in western Europe at least, were the Vikings. Based in Scandinavia, the Vikings sailed the oceans and rivers of Europe as far south as Italy, looting and pillaging whenever they could. "Never before has such terror appeared in

Britain as we have now suffered,"[6] mourned Alcuin of York in 789 after a particularly violent raid by a Viking band on England. Similar complaints could be heard in much of the rest of the continent.

The threat posed by the Vikings and other marauders was especially strong along the coasts and in rural areas. Given the Vikings' skill as soldiers and their general bloodthirstiness, even the larger cities had difficulty beating back a Viking invasion. In the countryside, defending against attack was essentially impossible. "Farms, villages and hamlets were isolated, more or less at the mercy of nature and vulnerable to outlaws, raiders and invaders,"[7] Lepage points out. The best, indeed the only, solution to this problem was fortification. A solid building could serve as a refuge for farmers who were under attack. The farmers' lands would likely still be despoiled and their houses flattened by the marauders, but a fort might save the lives of the people who hurried inside it when Viking ships appeared on the horizon.

Feudalism

The second change was the development of a new political and economic system in Europe in the early 800s, a system called feudalism. Under this system, Europe was divided among a number of important overlords, all of them members of the nobility and some of them kings. In turn, these overlords gave large sections of their land to lesser lords, who agreed to fight for the overlord as necessary. The lords' lands were known as estates, manors, or fiefs. Each fief was home not only to the noble and his family but also to many peasants, called serfs or vassals. The serfs were required to work for the nobleman, usually by growing crops. The lord offered the serfs military protection in exchange for their labor.

Politically speaking, though, the feudal system was unstable. Noblemen jockeyed endlessly with one another for wealth and power. In particular, they coveted each other's fiefs, and if they thought they could stage a successful attack on another lord and take his lands, they were likely to try. Nobles, one chronicler of the time wrote, "spend most of their time fighting and slaughtering their enemies."[8] The network of promises and obligations that defined feudal society, moreover, meant that if one lord or overlord attacked another, several more were honor bound to come to each participant's aid—thus escalating even minor conflicts. Because wars were so common under the feudal system, and because lords who lost the wars lost their land—the basic unit of wealth and status in feudal Europe—noblemen put great stress on defending their territory. A lord would face financial ruin if his enemies took his land.

Fortifications, then, made increasing sense as Europe moved into the feudal era. A well-built fortress could serve as a bulwark that protected against attack—and if it were imposing enough, it might dissuade enemies from starting a battle altogether. At the same time, noble families began finding it advantageous to move into the forts they built. In a time of shifting battle tactics, it seemed foolish for lords to live in poorly defended houses, which had been the norm earlier in the Middle Ages. Since the high walls of the fortress offered plenty of protection to soldiers, it made sense to design these new fortresses to house the nobility as well. The combination of defensive purposes and living quarters resulted in a new type of structure: the medieval castle.

WORDS IN CONTEXT

motte and bailey
A castle consisting of one or more buildings on a flat-topped hill and a wall surrounding them.

Motte and Bailey Construction

The forts of the 800s and 900s largely followed the same basic design, which produced the structures known today as motte and bailey castles, or simply motte and baileys. A motte is a raised piece of land with a flat top, and a bailey is an enclosure. First, workers would build the motte by creating a mound of earth and smoothing it flat. The size of mottes varied, but they were often quite large. Early mottes could measure 30 feet (9 m) tall, occasionally higher, though some were much shorter;

A painting from the late fifteenth century depicts peasants working outside a castle. Under feudalism the peasants worked for a lord who owned the land and the castle and in return offered the peasants protection.

and many were 100 feet (30 m) in diameter, sometimes much more. Building a motte, then, required many, many tons of earth—and given the limited technology of the time, also required great strength and stamina on the part of the laborers.

Usually the motte was surrounded by a wide ditch called a moat (the words *moat* and *motte* share a common origin). Ideally the ditch was a natural by product of digging up the earth to construct the raised platform that would form the motte. It seems likely, however, that most moats required further excavation to make them usable. The ditch was sometimes filled with water and sometimes not, but in either case it formed an extra barrier to an attacking army. In peacetime, removable wooden bridges allowed people to pass over the moat safely. As Laurence, a British clergyman, described Durham Castle in England around 1150, "The bridge is let down for egress [going out], and thus the way goes across the broad moat."[9] Once the motte and the ditch were completed, workers typically constructed one or more wooden structures on top of the motte. These buildings provided shelter for soldiers and nobles. They also provided a base from which sentries could scan the surrounding countryside in search of enemies. Sometimes these buildings were towers; sometimes they were single-story buildings, shorter but wider. Though many of the structures, especially those intended for soldiers, were little more than huts, constructed in haste and with any materials on hand, others were much more elaborate. Many mottes included a central tower, for example, which was roomy enough to house a noble family as well as a supply of weapons.

These buildings were strong, carefully designed, and well fortified; and though they were constructed of timber rather than stone, they were nonetheless imposing. Certainly observers of the time were impressed by the sight of a sturdy tower on top of the motte. "On this open space the [tower] is seated like a queen," Laurence boasted about Durham Castle. "From its threatening height, it holds all that it sees as its own."[10] And even if the tower were not as strong as it seemed from a distance, it was still effective. Nobles looking for fiefs to attack tended to seek out those that appeared to be poorly defended. Simply by building a tower that looked solid, then, nobles could discourage armies from attacking their holdings.

Walls of Wood

While the buildings were being constructed, work was also beginning on the bailey, or outer enclosure. Workers created this part of the castle by building a wooden fence around the motte. The fence provided some protection from enemies; it also served to encircle and mark off the space around the castle. The fences were not especially high. Nor were they much thicker than the diameter of a single log. Indeed, they probably had more in common with a stockade fence in frontier America than with the thick, strong castle walls of the 1200s or 1300s. Nonetheless, they presented a barrier to an attacking force, and as with the presence of a tower, sometimes the existence of a barrier was enough to convince an invading army to attack some other manor. The strongest of the wooden walls, moreover, stood up quite well against the spears, arrows, and swords of the early Middle Ages.

The castle known as a motte and bailey (pictured) consisted of a raised, earthen mound and an enclosed courtyard surrounded by a moat that was sometimes, but not always, filled with water. The greatest threat to this type of castle was fire, as the buildings were all made from timber.

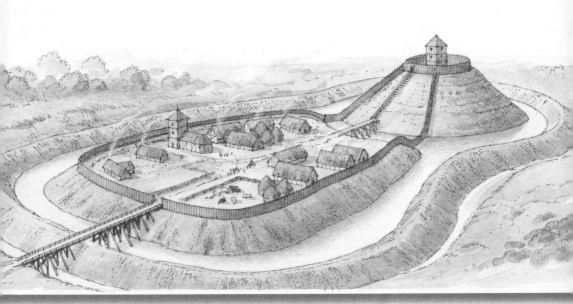

CASTLES AND THE BAYEUX TAPESTRY

The Bayeux Tapestry is one of the great treasures of medieval England. It is a long piece of cloth that has been embroidered with scenes from the Middle Ages. Its emphasis is on the events that led up to the capture of the English throne by the Norman king William the Conqueror in 1066. The tapestry, which was probably created in the 1070s, includes about fifty scenes depicting battles, coronations, travel, and much more.

The tapestry has rightly been celebrated as a remarkable artistic achievement, and it is an invaluable source of information about the conquest of England. The tapestry, however, also contains important information about medieval social, cultural, and architectural practices. It depicts the sorts of clothing that the people of the time wore, for instance, and some of the embroidery reveals interesting details about medieval agriculture and transportation.

In particular, some of what is known today about motte and baileys comes from the Bayeux Tapestry. Several of the tapestry's frames show castles of the time, either as the main part of the scene or occasionally in the background. One scene, for example, shows the Normans building a motte and bailey at the town of Hastings. Though the scenes were not intended to be representations of the actual events, it makes sense to conclude that the pictures reflect the basics of what the castles looked like.

The wooden walls, however, were not sufficient to ward off attacks from heavier armaments. They could be breached, for example, by the use of a battering ram—a long cylindrical object such as the trunk of a large tree. Attacking forces would smash the ram into the wall repeatedly until it broke into pieces or collapsed altogether. Then the invaders would rush into the bailey. Of course, sometimes the defenders could prevent the attackers from coming close enough to the wall for the battering ram to do its work. Some early medieval armies got around this problem by launching projectiles from a distance. A steady stream of boulders hitting a sensitive spot along the wall would soon damage and destroy the barricade.

The greatest danger to these early castles, however, did not come from a standard weapon. Instead, it came from fire. Because the walls and the buildings of a motte and bailey were made of timber, they were highly flammable. On a dry day a fire would quickly spread from one part of the castle wall to the next. High winds could make it almost impossible to extinguish the flames, and the castle might be destroyed. If invaders could move up to the castle's edge, they could kindle a fire directly by the wall. If not, archers could shoot flaming arrows at the wall in the hope of setting the wall aflame, or giant throwing machines could be used to hurl burning bales of hay at the fortifications for the same purpose.

Despite their vulnerabilities, the motte and bailey castles were generally effective at keeping invaders at bay, and they remained in regular use for many years. Even into the 1100s, the wooden motte and bailey represented a common design for medieval castles. The nobles in one region, a chronicler noted in about 1130, "raise a mound of earth as high as they can and surround it with a ditch as high and deep as possible. The top of this mound they completely enclose with a palisade [fence] of hewn logs bound close together like a wall, with towers set in its circuit so far as the site permits."[11] Given the passage of time and the new knowledge acquired by builders, these castles were no doubt stronger and more extensive than the castles of the 900s. But they still used the same basic materials and the same simple design as the earlier castles.

> **WORDS IN CONTEXT**
> palisade
> *A fence made of wood and used for defensive purposes.*

Changing Designs

That would change, however. By the end of the 1100s, and in many cases before, castles were increasingly being built in new ways. Stone, which was sturdier and much less vulnerable to fire than timber, began to come into favor. Castles grew larger inside and out, with more rooms, higher walls, and new features enabling a castle's defenders to better fight off the enemy. By the end of the 1200s, the new designs had mostly overtaken the wooden motte and bailey standard of an earlier time. Still, the connection between the later castles and their earlier counterparts is clear. From the Roman fortresses that preceded the medieval era to the imposing structures of the late Middle Ages, the castle evolved slowly but inexorably, with each new method, design, or material developing from the ones before. The story of the medieval castle is the story of this slow but steady evolution.

CHAPTER TWO

Gates, Rooms, and Towers

There was no such thing as a "typical" medieval castle. A castle's size, shape, and layout depended on a variety of factors: the owner's financial situation, the experience of the men who built the structure, the materials available where the castle was built, and much more. Castles varied according to region, too, with each part of Europe having its own distinctive building style. And of course castle design changed as the medieval period wore on. As a result, the castles of the Middle Ages differed considerably. A castle of the 1300s constructed by a wealthy Bulgarian king, say, was not at all the same as a castle of the 900s built by a much less-well-off lord in Scotland.

Nonetheless, by the last few centuries of the medieval period, castle designs and construction techniques had become increasingly standardized. By the 1100s Europeans had been building and using castles for several hundred years. They had seen firsthand which materials and config-urations worked to keep invaders at bay— and which did not. Accordingly, Europeans adopted the features that were effective and rejected or modified the rest. The castles of the later Middle Ages, then, while far from alike in every particular, did share many important characteristics. From sturdy walls to stately towers, from the portcullis that blocked

WORDS IN CONTEXT
portcullis
Latticed gate made of wood and metal.

the building's entrance to the narrow windows that enabled archers to shoot from a position of safety, the castles of the later medieval era had a great deal in common.

The Castle Wall

The most critical part of any castle was its wall. The wall was in a sense the skin of the castle: it kept the invaders out and protected the people inside. Although wooden castle walls were common into the 1100s, the later medieval period was better known for constructing walls of stone. Stone was much less vulnerable to fire than timber and could usually be made stronger as well. The main downside of stone was that it was often difficult and expensive to obtain. Unless a castle was built directly beside a quarry, stone had to be transported long distances at great cost. And even if a quarry were nearby, it took considerable work—and time—to carve the rock into usable stone. Still, for many nobles, the defensive benefits of stone outweighed the drawbacks. That was especially true as time passed and it became evident that stone castles withstood assault better than wooden ones.

Because the castle walls were so important, builders took pains to make the walls as strong as possible. If it was necessary for financial reasons to skimp on some part of the castle design, nobles invariably chose to cut corners in the interior rather than in the construction of the walls. As a result, the castle walls of the later Middle Ages were truly massive. Thickness, in particular, was essential if a castle was to stand up to repeated attacks from battering rams or similar weapons. Beginning in the 1100s most castles had walls at least 7 feet (2 m) thick, and many castle walls were far thicker even than that. At Chepstow Castle in Wales, for example, the walls measured 20 feet (6 m) thick—more than the length of an SUV today. And some parts of the wall at Borl Castle, in what is now Croatia, were 40 feet (12 m) thick.

Height was important as well. The higher a castle wall, the more time and effort it took for attackers to reach the top. The extra effort

The massive walls of Chepstow Castle in Wales (pictured) offered protection from repeated attacks from battering rams and other such weapons. Thick, high walls were a common feature of castles from the 1100s on.

wearied and weakened the invading force, and the extra time gave the defenders more opportunity to respond. High walls also allowed the castle's archers to shoot from a higher angle while still being protected from enemy fire; this was an added advantage for the defenders. Some later medieval castles had walls that were only about 15 to 20 feet (4.6 m to 6 m) high, but the walls of the stronger castles typically measured about 30 feet (9 m) in height and sometimes more. The wall of England's Framlingham Castle reached 40 feet (12 m) above the ground. In general, as the medieval era wore on and weaponry improved, the walls of newly constructed castles grew ever thicker and higher.

Crenels, Arrowloops, and Towers

Castle walls were rarely uniform in height, however. Most later medieval castles—and many earlier ones as well—had large gaps or indentations on the upper part of their walls. These gaps, known as crenels, gave castles their distinctive notched profile and lowered the height of the wall by a few feet wherever they were placed. Building a wall with crenels was known as crenellation, and the top of a crenellated wall was called the castle's parapet. Behind the parapet was a walkway or platform which ran the length of the wall and which was accessible from ground level by a staircase or ladder. This platform enabled soldiers to stand behind the parapet and fight the enemy from the top of the walls. Though crenellations were decorative, their primary purpose was defensive. Archers on the parapet could shoot arrows through the crenels, then duck back behind the safety of the wall before the enemy could respond.

WORDS IN CONTEXT

parapet
The top of a castle wall.

Many castle walls also featured smaller gaps called arrowloops. These were narrow slits, most often vertical, which the builders placed at various spots within the walls. The arrowloops served the same basic purpose as the crenellations: They allowed bowmen inside the castle to fire arrows at the enemy without risk to themselves. Compared to crenels, arrowloops had both advantages and disadvantages. The arrowloop was so thin that it could be difficult to see the enemy clearly or to fire in any direction but straight ahead. On the other hand, a well-aimed arrow launched toward the parapets might strike an unsuspecting archer who looked through a crenel at the wrong moment, whereas the arrowloops were so narrow that a castle bowman aiming through the loop was almost completely safe from harm.

Just as crenels cut into castle walls, lowering their height in places, later castles often had towers along the walls that made the barrier taller. Typically the towers rose another 10 feet (3 m) or so above the rest of the wall. Like the wall itself, the top of a tower often included crenellations. The added height of these towers made them especially good lookout posts. If an invasion was expected, a sentry stationed in the tower could see an army coming and alert the castle's garrison long before the enemy arrived. Similarly, during an attack a lookout could report the positions of the invading army to the soldiers below. The towers were also used by sharpshooters, who benefited by aiming their arrows from an even higher vantage point than provided by the walls.

In nearly all early medieval castles and many late ones as well, the outer wall was the only defense against attack. Beginning around 1200, however, large castles were often built with a second

Design Elements of a Tower

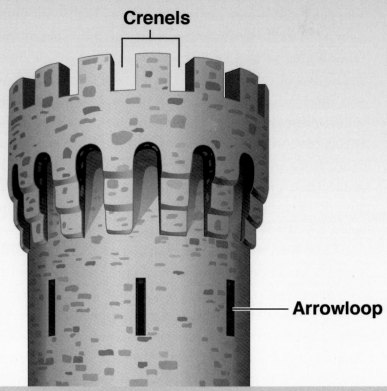

Crenels

Arrowloop

Source: All About Castles, "Glossary of Terms." www.allcrusades.com.

set of walls inside the outer rim. In case the enemy pushed through the outer walls, the castle's defenders could retreat inside the inner walls and continue the fight. The inner walls of these castles were usually stronger and higher than the outer walls—one historian describes the inner wall of Beaumaris Castle in Wales as "massively fortified" and "the ultimate strength of the castle."[12] Castles of this type are often called concentric castles, and the double-wall construction made them particularly difficult to conquer—and extremely expensive to build. Next to Beaumaris, the Krak des Chevaliers, a castle in Syria, is probably the best-known example of this type of construction.

The Gate

Even the strongest, best-fortified castle walls had a major weakness, however. This was the castle gate, an opening in the wall to allow the passage of people and supplies. Every castle had at least one gate, and larger castles sometimes had more than one. Gates were vulnerable because they were the only part of the castle's perimeter that lacked a thick wall, making them an appealing target for an invading army. Indeed, when a castle fell to an enemy, it was often because the attackers came through the gate. In 1306, an eyewitness reported, Greek soldiers attacking a Turkish castle "proceeded to break down the main doors, meeting with no resistance from anyone. And once the doors had been sundered, they made their entry, slaying and destroying all they found before them."[13] Dozens of other castles in and around Europe were conquered in precisely this way.

To be sure, the gates were built to make an attack difficult. Often they featured heavy wooden doors that could be closed and locked in the event of an invasion. Many also were equipped with a wood-and-iron grating called a portcullis, which could be lowered behind the gate and secured to form another barrier. Some castles had two portcullises spaced along a corridor. Defenders would open the portcullis nearest the gate and shut the one further back, allowing attackers to

A LICENSE TO CRENELLATE

Though lords in medieval Europe had a great deal of autonomy, they were at least in theory subject to kings and other monarchs, and the laws and customs of their countries often required them to seek the monarch's permission before undertaking certain actions. In England, for example, medieval barons who wished to build castles were forced to obtain what historians call a license to crenellate. They were not allowed to construct fortifications of any kind unless they had obtained the consent of their monarch or another powerful national leader. Those who built castles without permission could have their property confiscated.

Some licenses to crenellate survive today. One example from 1282, written by Edward I, runs as follows: "Our beloved and loyal Stephen of Penchester and Margaret his wife may fortify and crenellate their house at Allington in the County of Kent with a wall of stone and lime, and that they and their heirs may hold it, thus fortified and crenellated, in perpetuity." Once the additions were complete, the building was known as Allington Castle.

Quoted in Lise Hull, *Britain's Medieval Castles*. Westport, CT: Praeger, 2005, p. 128.

storm down the corridor to the second portcullis. Once they reached it, the defenders would close the first portcullis, ensnaring the army between the two. "The walls of the tunnel between the portcullises [were] pierced with arrow loops from which the defenders could fire at the trapped intruders,"[14] notes one modern source. Warwick Castle in England is one example of a fortress equipped with this rather fiendish set of double portcullises.

Castle gates had other built-in protections as well. Chief among these were devices known as murder holes. In many castles, a small room jutted out from the castle wall directly above the gate. The floors of such rooms included one or more circular holes. Archers could shoot the attackers through the holes as the invaders tried to knock down the castle door. Alternatively, defenders could use the holes to drop rocks, molten lead, or boiling water on the enemy. As one historian writes, the defenders of the castle most often "selected the least pleasant possible items"[15] to drop on the soldiers below. At the very least, the rain of objects and liquids from above could slow the attackers; at best, they might seriously injure or even kill the enemy, saving the castle from defeat. More murder holes were placed inside the gate, allowing the defenders a second chance even if the gate were breached.

Indeed, the area behind the gate in some castles was designed specifically to confuse, harass, and disorient any attackers who beat down the door. As Jean-Denis Lepage writes, many castles featured "deceiving elements and cunning traps concealed in unexpected places such as hidden pits in floors, dead-end staircases, fake posterns [exits to the outside], genuine secret passages from which the defenders might sally forth upon intruders, [and] labyrinthine corridors."[16] How often these devices proved effective is uncertain, but their presence in so many castles testifies to the creativity of castle builders—and to the desire of castle owners to gain an advantage in any way they could.

Just as with the simple motte and bailey construction of the earliest castles, later medieval castles frequently used dry ditches or water-filled moats as another way to limit access to the castle. Indeed, by the 1100s only those castles built on hilltops and rocky outcroppings did not routinely include a moat. Invaders preferred to charge directly at the castle from level ground, but a moat forced attackers to climb across a ditch or make their way through water to reach their goal. In either case, the moat blocked soldiers' progress, making the invading army vulnerable to counterattack by archers in the parapets. In some cases, launching an offensive through the waters of a moat could sicken soldiers as well. When under attack, defenders were known to throw human waste or rotting corpses of animals into the moat to further dissuade opposing forces from trying to cross it.

The Bailey and the Keep

The castle walls and gates protected a wide variety of other spaces. The specific spaces varied widely from one castle to the next and from one era to another, but as with the walls and gates, certain interior features were common to many of the largest and most important medieval castles. Most late medieval castles, for example, had a bailey, the open area or courtyard behind the wall that was a prominent feature in early medieval castles. Smaller castles typically had just one bailey, but larger castles often had two, three, or even more. By the later Middle Ages, baileys were put to a variety of uses. These included drilling grounds for soldiers, grazing spaces for farm animals, and meeting spots where people in the castle complex could socialize.

In the center of the bailey most castles had a sturdy, well-fortified tower, most often made of stone. This was known as the keep or sometimes the donjon. If the wall was the skin of the castle, then the keep was the castle's heart. Described by Frances Gies and Joseph Gies as "lofty, formidable, threatening, and . . . enduring monuments of the age,"[17] keeps had a dual purpose. On the one hand, the keep was a living space, with the interior made as comfortable as possible for the nobleman and his family. On the other hand, it was the last line of defense for the castle's residents. If the walls of the castle were breached, defenders could retreat to the keep to continue the fight as best they could. The odds that an army trapped in the keep would emerge victorious were not great; but a well-built keep could at the least hold attackers at bay for some time.

Keeps varied in size and shape from castle to castle. Most were square, rectangular, or round, but other shapes were possible too. Trim Castle in Ireland had a keep with twenty sides, for instance, and the keep of the Château d'Etampes in France was a quatrefoil, similar to a four-leaf clover. The largest keeps measured approximately 100 feet by 100 feet (30 m by 30 m), or about the space covered by a Major League Baseball infield. Like castle walls, keeps were built to make entry difficult for invaders. At Dover Castle in England, the walls of

⬡ HYGIENE

One of the more intractable problems in medieval Europe had to do with hygiene. People who lived in cities and towns typically tossed their garbage into the streets, and the people who lived in castles were no different. Especially during wartime, garbage tended to pile up in the baileys and other common areas of medieval castles. The trash attracted insects, rats, and other creatures and often led to the spread of disease. On many occasions epidemics sped through the populations of castles, sickening and killing many of the people; the piles of garbage likely played a role in these outbreaks.

Some castles were built with a partial solution to the problem, at least where disposal of human waste was concerned. This was the garderobe, or toilet. Though modern flush toilets were unknown in medieval Europe, many castles contained small closets with holes carved into the floor. The holes in turn were connected to chutes designed to carry waste away from the castle's living quarters. The ultimate destination of these chutes varied. The contents sometimes drained into a storage area in or below the castle's basement but could also pour directly into the moat. While the garderobes could not remove human waste from the castle entirely, they did at least reduce the risk of disease by pushing it away from the places where people were most likely to spend their time.

the keep were 20 feet (6 m) thick and rose to a height of 80 (24 m) feet. "The keep rises . . . into thin air," marveled a medieval observer at another English castle, "strong within and without, well fitted for its work."[18]

Most large keeps consisted of three or four floors, though some had more; the keep at the Château de Vincennes in France had six. For the most part the rooms of the keep were meant for the noble family that owned the castle. Dover Castle included several large halls which lords used for entertaining and conducting business, and there were private spaces as well. At the French castle of

Ardres, one observer reported in the late 1100s, the second floor consisted mainly of "the great chamber in which the lord and his wife slept." Personal servants of the nobility were often housed in the keep too, as was the case at Ardres: "Adjoining [the great chamber] was a private room," the writer continued, "the dormitory of the waiting maids."[19]

Other Structures

In addition to the keep, the castle grounds included several lower and smaller buildings as well. Some noble families decided they wanted a larger great hall than could be housed in the keep, for instance, so they constructed a separate building strictly for that purpose. Goodrich Castle in Wales is one structure that features this arrangement. Castles of the Middle Ages also had buildings where commoners lived and worked. Artisans, for instance, often lived in small frame houses which were decently built and provided protection from the elements. Less fortunate residents of the castle, whether soldiers or peasants, slept in simple huts made of a mixture of mud, wood, and clay; these were easy to construct but not terribly effective at providing shelter. These houses and huts were usually found in the castle's bailey.

Animals, too, lived in castles, and they required shelter as well. Since horses were a major form of transport in medieval times, for example, castles included space for stables. Often the stables were separate buildings set in the bailey near the castle's entrance, but space limitations sometimes forced architects to be more creative. Chillon Castle in Switzerland is one of several in which the stables were most likely located below ground. Similarly, many castles kept pigs, cows, and other livestock. These animals provided milk and meat and were especially valuable if an enemy force surrounded the castle and prevented supplies from coming in. These animals were housed in small barns or pens in the bailey as well.

WORDS IN CONTEXT
oubliette
Prison cell with a single entrance and exit at the top.

Soldiers suffer a watery death as they battle for control of a castle in France in the 1400s. A water-filled moat often helped block the progress of an invading army—or drowned those unfortunate souls who fell into it.

Finally, castles often featured jail cells. Most commonly these were located in the towers or below the ground floor of the keep. These cells were used for prisoners of war, disobedient soldiers, or petty criminals who lived in the castle. While none of these cells could be called comfortable, the worst of them was a holding tank known as the *oubliette*. An oubliette had no door or windows, only a hatch in the ceiling. A prisoner was lowered through the trapdoor on a rope; then the hatch was closed and locked, leaving the prisoner in total darkness. If the captors felt generous they would occasionally send food and water down through the trap door by the same method, keeping the prisoner alive until the time came for his or her release. If the captors did not feel generous the prisoner was simply left to die.

Beauty and Comfort

A castle existed for practical reasons: for defense and for living space. That does not imply, though, that all the castle's features were purely utilitarian. Many castles included ornamentation for its own sake. Often these decorations were part of the castle's architecture. Stokesay Castle in England, for example, was built with arched windows in the main hall. The windows provided no defensive benefit but added to the charm and beauty of the room. At Caernarfon Castle in Wales, home to several British monarchs, "turrets of the tower most visible from the coastal approach were embellished with boldly carved eagles, the emblem of royalty."[20] And gargoyles, playful carved figures that served as drain spouts, were common features on the walls of many medieval castles.

Other decorative features were less permanent. The wealthiest castle owners decked out their suites with curtained beds and elaborate wall hangings. "The king's chamber was particularly well appointed," writes historian Jeffrey Singman about the room occupied by King Henry III of England at Dover Castle, "with glass windows [a rarity at the time] and wainscoted walls."[21] Many castles, especially toward the end of the medieval period, had flower gardens or fishponds to add visual appeal to the fortress. A few castle owners even added whimsical mechanical devices to entertain guests or to play practical jokes on them. "Statues in his garden squirted water on visitors when they walked past or squawked words at them like parrots," historian Barbara Tuchman writes about Robert of Artois, who lived in Hesdin Castle in France during the 1300s. "A trapdoor dropped the passersby onto a featherbed below."[22] Some of Robert's mechanical devices even imitated weather conditions. When the door to one room was opened, the unwary visitor was greeted with what appeared to be thunder, rain, or even snow.

Though every medieval castle was different, the similarities among them were perhaps even more noticeable. Especially toward the end of the Middle Ages a soldier, artisan, or lord who lived or worked at a castle in Portugal, say, would find a castle in Norway, Lebanon, or Slovenia to be quite familiar. Even if the features of the medieval castle varied, the basic purposes of every castle were the same: to provide a comfortable home for a noble family and to protect that family and their lands to every extent possible. It is no surprise that the people of medieval Europe found similar ways of meeting these goals throughout the period.

CHAPTER THREE

Constructing a Castle

Building a castle, especially in the later Middle Ages, was a massive undertaking. Medieval castles were only rarely completed in less than two years and often took considerably more time than that. Lords needed the labor of hundreds, sometimes thousands, of skilled and unskilled workers, along with expert artisans who could coordinate the work and make the process as efficient as possible. And the lord who owned the castle needed to have access to large sums of money to pay the workers and to buy raw materials when necessary. The construction of a medieval castle could only proceed, then, if three basic requirements were met: time, labor, and money.

But the building of a medieval castle was not just about practical considerations such as a lord's wealth and the size of the local labor force. Even by modern standards medieval castles were highly complex; they needed a first-rate defensive system, complete with parapets, a keep, a sturdy wall, and more. At the same time, castles required appealing living quarters for the lord and his family. To build castles that met both of these conditions, often in addition to being beautiful to look at, was an impressive achievement. The construction of a castle, then, required not only time and money but also ingenuity, craftsmanship, and a strong work ethic. Fortunately, the people of the Middle Ages had these traits.

Terrain, Height, and River Access

The first step in building any castle was to determine where to build it. Castles were not sited randomly but were built in places with particular military significance. Quite often, for instance, they were built on the tops of hills. The castle at Antioch in what is now Turkey, for example, was on a mountain about 1,000 feet (about 300 m) high. This placement forced invaders to launch attacks from below, which put them at a disadvantage; firing arrows upward was not as effective as firing them across level ground, and charging up a hill cost energy and strength. Moreover, placing castles in high places allowed defenders to see an attacking army as it approached. From Castle Coucy in northern France, Barbara Tuchman writes, "an observer could see the whole region as far as the forest of Compiegne thirty miles away, making Coucy [safe] against surprise."[23]

Castles frequently were built on the banks of rivers used by travelers and traders, too. This placement enabled the castle's occupants to control traffic along these routes, allowing friends to pass and preventing enemies from doing the same. The castle of Bouillon in France is an excellent example. Not only is it at a higher elevation than the surrounding countryside, but it overlooks the Semois River as well. Godfrey of Lotharingia, who controlled the castle in the late 1000s, was successful at keeping Bouillon out of the hands of his enemies—and launching attacks of his own on nearby lords from this nearly impenetrable fortress. Malbork Castle in Poland, built on the Nogat River, and Heidelberg Castle along the Rhin River in Germany are likewise famous for their riverbank locations.

The terrain was another consideration in deciding where to put a castle. The stones that were the basic building blocks of the late medieval castle were extremely heavy, so it was unwise to build on land that was less than solid. Trying to construct a castle in a swampy lowland, for example, was doomed to failure: the thicker the walls and towers were built, the sooner they would begin to sink into the ground.

WORDS IN CONTEXT

mason
Stoneworker.

Stonemasons and other workers labor over the materials to be used in building a castle. Castle construction required the efforts of hundreds, and sometimes thousands, of skilled and unskilled workers.

River access, dry land, a good view—each was an important factor in choosing where to build a medieval castle. The most significant concern of all, however, was drinking water. Castles had to have a reliable water supply within or at the very least just outside the castle walls; if the people inside had no access to water, they could not hold out against an attack. Though from a military perspective some hilltops and cliffs seemed to be ideal sites for castles, the lack of easy water access in these high places often forced builders to choose a lower but wetter spot instead. Nonetheless, a few intrepid builders found ways to construct elevated castles without compromising the need for water. Even without modern drills, for example, the builders at Beeston Castle in England dug a well that measured over 400 feet (122 m) deep.

Lords and Architects

Once a spot for a castle had been chosen, it was time to plan its construction. Exactly how this process worked is not entirely clear. In particular, it is often difficult to determine who was primarily responsible for designing the castle and its essential features—the thickness of the walls, the height of the towers, the layout of the rooms. Medieval society was stratified, and except for the few people at the top—kings, other lords, and bishops—individual accomplishments were rarely noted. As a result, most accounts of castle construction, especially in the early Middle Ages, conclude that just one man was responsible for the work: the lord who commissioned it. As one historian wryly notes, "Medieval chroniclers had no doubt about who deserved the credit for the great buildings of their age."[24]

Certainly lords were part of the process. Many of the nobles who commissioned castles were most likely active partners in designing them. If nothing else, the nobles were experts from a military perspective. They knew the size of their armies, they knew the strategies and tactics favored by their enemies, and they understood the geographic features of the castle's location. Most lords, moreover, had been involved in attacks on other castles and had clear ideas about what defenses worked—and what defenses did not. Finally, the lord knew how much money he had, giving him a strong incentive not to design more than he could afford to build. Given the lord's knowledge of these matters, it would have been odd indeed for him to stay out of the process altogether.

PLANS, MODELS, AND PARCHMENT

In modern times architects routinely sketch out designs for even the simplest of structures. It would make sense to assume that medieval castle designers drew plans as well, most likely on parchment—the best approximation of paper in medieval times. But there is considerable debate among architectural historians about whether they did. Very few plans for the buildings of the Middle Ages exist today, and the few that do are from cathedrals, not castles.

Some historians interpret lack of plans as evidence that castle designers of the time did not use drawings to record their ideas. Instead, these historians argue, architects kept designs in their heads and told workers what to do as they reached each step in the process. Other historians, in contrast, believe that architects did draw up plans. They attribute the lack of surviving drawings to the fact that parchment was rare and expensive, so the designs were erased at the end of each project, allowing the parchment to be reused.

There is some evidence, moreover, that master masons sometimes made three-dimensional models to display their ideas. These models are occasionally referenced in the descriptions of castle building at the time. As with drawings of plans, there is much that historians do not know about medieval models—how large they were, what they were made of, and how widespread the practice was. The lack of information may be frustrating, but the uncertainty is typical for a period when literacy was rare and photography did not yet exist.

Still, it is clear that even in the early part of the Middle Ages, much of the work of designing castles was done by experts hired for the occasion. Some of these men were referred to as architects; others were experienced stoneworkers called master masons. By 1100 their names begin to appear in the historical record. When William I of England wanted to build a castle in London, for example, he employed a French clergyman named Gundulf to serve as the main designer. As a modern writer describes him, Gundulf "was an emotional man, given to outbursts of weeping, which won him the disrespectful nickname 'the Wailing Monk.'"[25] Nonetheless, Gundulf had directed the

Malbork Castle in Poland (pictured) is situated along the Nogat River. Locating a castle on a river allowed the lord of the castle to control travel and trade as well as providing protection from enemy invaders.

construction of castles and cathedrals in the past, and he was a wise choice. Today, Gundulf is credited with designing the beginnings of the Tower of London, one of the world's most famous castles.

Master James

As time went on, architects became better recognized for their work. By the late 1200s several master masons were widely sought out by lords eager to build a state-of-the-art fortification. Among the most famous of these today is a man known as Master James of St. George. Born around 1230 in southern France, James designed at least a dozen castles in Wales and several more elsewhere. His works are admired for their symmetry, creativity, and overall beauty. In particular, James is credited with developing the concept of concentric castles— castles with both inner and outer walls. Beaumaris Castle in northern

Wales, considered by many to be his greatest achievement, has been called Great Britain's "most perfect example of symmetrical concentric planning."[26]

Master James's reputation as a castle designer in France evidently preceded him to Great Britain; he was almost certainly recruited by King Edward I of England specifically to design the castles in Wales. The evidence strongly suggests that Edward was pleased with James's work. Toward the end of James's career he was earning three shillings a day, or about the same as a craftsman might earn in a week and a half—and far more than the typical unskilled worker could hope to earn in a month. Indeed, Edward guaranteed that James's income would remain at that level for the rest of his life, an indication of the esteem in which the king held his employee.

In addition to planning castles, Master James and other designers were responsible for overseeing the building of each castle they planned. This work was similar to that of a modern-day construction manager or foreman. It seems clear that master masons enjoyed the power this aspect of their job afforded them. "He orders his men about," wrote clergyman Jacques de Vitry, describing what he perceived to be the typical master mason, "but rarely or never lends his own hand." Indeed, de Vitry noted, designers could be quite peremptory in their demands. "Pointing his walking stick," de Vitry explained, "[the master mason] directs, 'Cut here,' or 'Cut there.'"[27] Given the architect's high status, the workers hastened to do as they were told.

> **WORDS IN CONTEXT**
> peremptory
> *Dictatorial, rude in giving orders.*

But on large projects, managing workers took nearly all of a master mason's time. Master James, for instance, was often in charge of several thousand laborers. These included skilled workers, such as blacksmiths, carpenters, and stonemasons, along with unskilled laborers, such as carters, diggers, and woodcutters. "We have needed 400 masons," Master James wrote regarding the workforce at one castle site, "together with 2000 less skilled workmen." The ranks of workers, James noted, also included "200 quarrymen; 30 smiths

THE KRAK DES CHEVALIERS

One of the most famous and imposing of all medieval castles was the Krak des Chevaliers in what is now Syria. Though located in the Middle East, the castle was built by eleventh-century Europeans as part of the Crusades, an attempt by Christians to reclaim the Holy Land from Muslim control. In the early 1000s the crusaders took large swaths of territory from Islamic forces. To protect their conquests the crusaders constructed a new castle—the Krak des Chevaliers, or the fortress of the knights.

The Krak des Chevaliers is widely admired in part for its design and beauty. Built on a hill, the castle dominates the landscape around it. T.E. Lawrence, a British figure of the early 1900s better known as Lawrence of Arabia, described it as the "most wholly admirable castle in the world," and other observers over the years have agreed with him. The structure utilizes a double-wall construction, which allowed it to repel many attacks in the years after it was constructed. Indeed, the Krak des Chevaliers was among the last crusader possessions to fall to Muslim armies. The castle also has great historical significance. Because it belonged at various times to both European Christians and Middle Eastern Muslims, it blends both cultures in its architectural features and interior design. Today, the Krak des Chevaliers is classified as a World Heritage Site by the United Nations, a designation that recognizes and honors the castle's great architectural, cultural, and historic value.

Quoted in Kelly DeVries, *Medieval Military Technology*. Peterborough, ON: Broadview, 1992, p. 231.

[blacksmiths]; and carpenters for putting in the joists and floor boards and other necessary jobs."[28] Managing all these men and coordinating their efforts took enormous amounts of time and energy.

The castle designer had one further responsibility: He kept track of the money being spent on the project. In particular, he needed to make sure the workers got paid on time, and he had to justify all his expenses to the lord who owned the castle—and more important, to the lord's treasurer. "The men's pay has been and still is very much in arrears [behind]," Master James wrote at one point to King Edward's accountant, "and we are having the greatest difficulty in keeping them because they simply have nothing to live on."[29] A medieval architect, then, needed not only good design skills; he also needed to be a good manager of employees, to have a head for finance, and to possess the ability to be diplomatic or forceful with his superiors as the occasion demanded. It seems likely that Master James earned his salary.

The Building Process

Once the plan of the castle had been decided, it was time to start building. The first step was to bring in carpenters and other workers to put together temporary housing for the laborers, along with workshops for the craftsmen who would join the project later on. After that, workers typically laid out the outline of the castle, first with stakes and ropes, then with a wooden fence that provided basic security as the castle took shape. In some cases, the land was already suitable for building a fortress and needed no further work to prepare it for construction. In other cases, though, hillocks needed to be knocked down or ditches had to be filled. Laborers evened out the land as necessary. Likewise, some castles required a foundation, which meant that diggers had to create a huge hole with picks and shovels.

While all this was going on at the castle site, other laborers would be hard at work cutting pieces of stone from rock quarries. Skilled stoneworkers then used hammers and chisels to carve the stones into the appropriate size and shape. Ideally the stones would all have the same dimensions, which would make it easier for workers to set them in rows and layers without gaps or overlaps. Once the stones were shaped to the master mason's satisfaction, they would be placed in carts and brought to the work site—a difficult task, given the weight of the stones, and one that usually required the pulling power of horses or other draft animals.

When the stones reached the castle site, workers set them up in two parallel rows. One row would become the inner edge of the castle wall, and the other would form the outside edge. Laborers used a mortar

The Concentric Castle

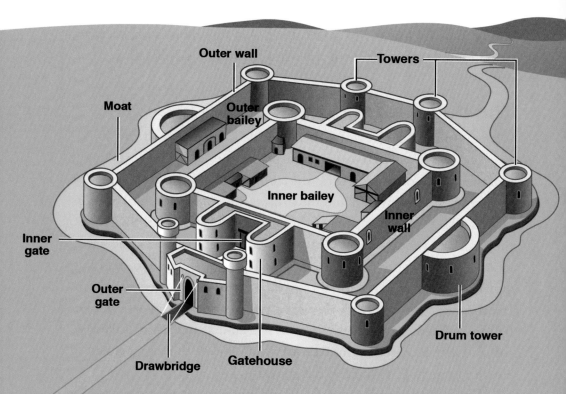

Source: Encyclopedia Britannica, Inc., "Concentric Castle," 2006.

made of water, soil, and lime to fasten the stones end to end in each row. Once the bottom layer of stones was complete, work would begin on the second layer, with mortar serving this time to glue the layers together. When the walls had risen three or four feet (about 1 m), the space between them would be filled with rubble—random pieces of stone mixed with mortar. This connected the two edges and created the base for the completed wall. Then the process would begin again, raising the walls another three to four feet (about 1 m) at a time until the structure was the desired height.

Scaffolding, Roofs, and the Interior

That system was effective in the early stages of construction, but before long the wall grew too tall for workers to reach up to the top. When that happened, laborers made scaffolding out of wood and placed it beside the wall. The scaffolding had a platform where workers could stand to place the stones. Scaffolds were built with ramps as well, which not only permitted the workers to climb to the platforms but also made it possible to drag the heavy stones to the top. By adding more levels to the scaffold, it could be made to rise higher and higher, until the platform reached the planned height of the wall. A similar process was used to build the towers, the keep, and the inner wall, assuming that the castle had one.

Building the roof was another important task. Most castles had roofs made of wood rather than stone, which was too heavy and therefore likely to collapse. The wood was typically covered with some other material to strengthen it and keep moisture away from the timber. The specific materials depended on what was available in the immediate area as well as on the economic resources of the lord who owned the castle. Some of the bigger medieval castles used a thin layer of metal to cover the roof. A list of materials purchased to build Aberystwyth Castle in Wales, for example, includes the entry "2 ½ loads of lead for roofing the . . . tower and other 'houses' in the castle."[30] Less elaborate castles used thatch, oak, slate, or even clay as coverings for their roofs.

Upon completion of the walls and the exterior shells of the keep and towers, workers shifted their focus to the castle's interior. The first task was generally to construct floors and ceilings. Masons began by placing stones called corbels at ceiling height along the inside of a building's walls. One end of the corbels projected into the interior of the space. Workers then rested heavy wooden beams on the corbels, spanning the distance across the room. These formed the foundation for floors made of wooden planks set side by side and nailed to the beams to set them firmly into place. Masons also constructed fireplaces and chimneys. Fireplaces set directly in the wall, in particular, were a twelfth-century innovation; according to Frances Gies and Joseph Gies, the innovation was "immediately and widely copied"[31] for other buildings as well.

Time, Men, and Money

The time involved in building a castle varied. Construction often halted during the winter, especially in northern Europe; daylight was scarce, snow interfered with the work, and the cold temperatures froze the mortar used to connect the blocks of stone. Thus, work crews generally went home in December and did not return till March or April. Even so, if work crews hurried, they could complete a small castle in one season; Château Gaillard in France was built in a matter of months. Longer time frames were more common, however. Chilham Castle in Great Britain took three years to complete, the building of Dover Castle stretched out across ten summers, and Beaumaris Castle was under construction for thirty-five years—and was never actually completed.

WORDS IN CONTEXT

corbel

A piece of stone or wood that juts from a wall and holds beams or other weights.

The length of time it took to construct a fortress made for great expense. Skilled workers demanded decent wages, and although unskilled workers were paid very little per day, the number of men required to build even small castles—and the number of days their labor was needed—served to inflate payroll very quickly. Sometimes nobles saved money by using their serfs as laborers; since these peasants were legally bound to serve them, they could be paid even less than the prevailing rate for unskilled workers or forced to work for nothing at all. Using the labor of serfs, however, was costly in other ways. Peasants who worked full-time building a castle—and it was indeed a full-time job—could not grow crops, meaning that the nobleman would have to bring food in from outside which was costly.

Nobles could sometimes escape labor charges by importing materials from elsewhere. Some English castles were built using stone brought in from France, for example. But that served only to shift the expense: instead of paying skilled men to cut the stones, these nobles had to pay for the materials. If the cost of shipping heavy stones is added in, it seems doubtful that this strategy saved any money whatever. No matter how many corners a noble tried to cut, then, the reality was that castles were extremely costly—especially the large stone fortresses of the later Middle Ages. To build about a dozen castles in Wales, for example, Edward I spent an estimated £100,000 (English pounds)—the very rough equivalent of $1 billion today.

These inflated costs reveal the huge importance of castles to the noblemen of the Middle Ages. Despite the expense involved in constructing a castle, despite the stress of managing hundreds or thousands of workers, despite the years the project could take, the wealthy nobles of medieval Europe recognized that it was still better to go through the process than not. Though a castle took many months to build and carried a colossal price tag, the alternative to constructing one was unthinkable. A nobleman who did not invest in a sturdy castle was a nobleman who would soon lose his land, his wealth, his status—and very likely his life. Compared to that fate, the difficulties of building a castle seemed minor indeed.

CHAPTER FOUR

Castles and Warfare

The primary purpose of a castle was defense. Its effectiveness was measured not by the spaciousness of the rooms, by the cost of the roof, or by the time it took to construct, but by its ability to keep enemies out. Given the medieval enthusiasm for warfare, nearly all castles were battle-tested, and many were attacked multiple times over the years. Castle builders became increasingly good at determining which architectural features were most likely to help defeat a prolonged attack. As a result, designs, materials, and building methods steadily improved as time passed, and castles became stronger and more difficult to capture.

The improvements in castle defense did not mean that conquering a castle became impossible, however. Castle builders were not the only people studying warfare during the Middle Ages. Attackers were every bit as determined to breach castle walls as the castle defenders were to keep them out. As castle defenses developed, soldiers came up with new tactics and technologies to defeat the new defensive features. Throughout the medieval period, then, attackers and defenders were locked in a constant struggle for supremacy. The development of castles over time was driven by the strengths and weaknesses they revealed in times of war.

Medieval Warfare

Warfare in medieval Europe could take place for almost any reason, real or imagined. A lord's identity was quite often tightly linked to his willingness to fight, and honor was not an abstract concept; a lord perceived to be avoiding battle was marked as a coward. That was true even if a fight seemed likely to settle nothing and result only in the needless deaths of soldiers and commanders alike. Indeed, enthusiasm for war was so deeply ingrained in medieval European culture that King John of Bohemia took part in a 1346 battle despite having been blinded several years earlier. Unsurprisingly, he was killed in action—but was praised by both sides as a great warrior. As a contemporary chronicler put it, John "fought valiantly."[32]

Virtually all noblemen of the Middle Ages had a standing army, then, prepared to attack or defend as their commanders dictated. A lord who wished to stage an invasion would simply order his army to the site of the enemy's castle. On some occasions the invading force immediately launched an attack. Perhaps surprisingly, however, attacking armies often did not actually fight, at least not at first. Rather, they started by besieging, or laying siege to, the castle. This involved surrounding the castle, making it impossible for people or supplies to move either into the castle or out of it. If that could be accomplished, the attackers only had to wait. Eventually the defenders would consume all the food they had stored in the castle. Unable to replenish their stock, they would have to surrender—or starve.

The outcomes of medieval sieges varied. In some cases those inside the castle surrendered within a few hours. That was especially true when an imbalance in the sizes of the two armies was obvious or when the castle had fallen into disrepair and the defenders knew its walls could easily be breached. It also happened when the defenders believed they would be killed if they put up a fight but hoped for kinder treatment if they surrendered quickly. In 1037 soldiers in Château de Chinon in France gave up as soon as they were besieged by the armies of Fulk III, the Count of Anjou—a decision doubtless helped along by Fulk's reputation, described by a modern historian as a "plunderer, murderer, robber, and swearer of false oaths."[33]

The 1037 siege of Château de Chinon in France ended almost as soon as it began, probably because of the terrifying reputation of the attacking noble. The same castle experienced later sieges including one depicted in this fourteenth-century artwork.

Holding Out

More often, however, the besieged defenders in the castle refused to give up so easily. In part this decision was based on the difficulty of completely surrounding a castle. Especially in rough, hilly regions, defenders could sometimes move in and out of the castle without being seen, enabling them to restock caches of food and weapons.

Castles that were built on seacoasts were particularly hard to besiege successfully. In 1294 an army led by Welshman Madoc ap Llywelyn besieged Harlech Castle in Wales. Madoc's men prevented goods from reaching the castle's garrison by land. But Harlech was on the ocean, and Madoc could not stop the flow of supplies to the castle by sea. He eventually had to call off the siege.

On other occasions sieges ended due to dissension in the attacking army. In July 1410 a joint force from Lithuania and Poland besieged a Prussian fortress. Though outnumbered, the defenders decided to hold out. That was a wise decision, as the invaders proved unprepared to maintain an extended siege. Morale among the soldiers was already low, in part because they had not been paid, and as harvest time approached many were eager to go home to tend to their crops. An outbreak of disease further reduced the number of able fighters in the Lithuanian-Polish army. The siege was called off in mid-September.

And once in a while a siege was broken due to the trickery of those inside the castle. A particularly intriguing incident of this took place at Pembroke Castle in Wales. In 1096 Pembroke was held by Norman forces from France under the command of Gerald of Windsor. That year, however, a Welsh army besieged the castle, and the Normans ran low on food. Knowing they would soon starve, Gerald hit on a plan. "He had four swine in the castle," writes a historian; "he cut them in pieces, and threw them over to the besiegers."[34] Seeing this waste of food, the Welsh concluded that the Normans had plenty remaining. Fooled into believing that the Normans were still powerful, they abandoned the siege.

Finally, defenders sometimes held out even against great odds if they anticipated the arrival of reinforcements. Those inside the castle could ration what food they had for days or even weeks, as long as they believed that help was on the way. Sometimes reinforcements did arrive in time to attack the invaders and drive them away. In 1294, soon after Madoc ap Llywelyn unsuccessfully besieged Harlech Castle, Madoc and his men trapped

WORDS IN CONTEXT
reinforcements
Newly arrived soldiers ready to join an existing battle.

England's King Edward I inside Conwy Castle in Wales. This siege lasted two months and might have forced a surrender if not for the timely arrival of soldiers loyal to Edward in January 1295. Waiting did not always prove effective, however. Often reinforcements never did arrive, forcing the defenders to give up.

Using Force

If an attacking army could not completely surround a castle, then invaders needed to use force to capture it. By the later medieval era armies had developed dozens of possible lines of attack, each designed to exploit a possible weakness in the castle's defenses. Some of these tactics were straightforward, others much more subtle. Whether they succeeded or failed, the attempts to take over castles during the Middle Ages almost always resulted in copious bloodshed and death, usually on both sides. "One [soldier] falls with gushing entrails, one with his throat cut," an observer of an assault on a French castle wrote enthusiastically, "there a thigh is shattered by a staff, here brains are scattered with a club."[35]

One common method of attack involved the use of throwing devices, known as catapults. The basic design of the catapult was known to the ancient Greeks and Romans. By medieval times there was a variety of them, each a different size and shape, including trebuchets, ballistas, mangonels, and springalds. Each of these machines had a timber frame and a long piece of wood, known as the catapult's beam or arm. One end of the arm was equipped with a sling that formed a basket. The attackers placed boulders or other objects into the basket and then launched the missiles at the castle, typically by releasing ropes or by means of a sophisticated system of counterweights.

Medieval catapults were highly effective. The sturdiest among them could throw objects weighing up to 300 pounds (136 kg),

THE TREBUCHET

No one knows exactly where the catapult system called a trebuchet developed. Some historians have called it a medieval innovation, while others trace its roots to classical Greece or Rome or, occasionally, to China. What is certain is that around the year 1200, Europeans made several important changes to the trebuchet's design to make it more accurate and powerful. One of these was switching from a system in which soldiers released the trebuchet's arm to a new design in which counterweights played the most important part. Historians Frances Gies and Joseph Gies describe the counterweight as "a hopper filled with earth or stone, specified in one source as 'nine feet across and twelve feet deep.'" The Gieses go on to describe the process of firing the remodeled trebuchet as follows:

> The machine's arm was mounted asymmetrically on a fulcrum, with the short end, pointing toward the target, given the counterweight. The long end, wound back by a winch, was released by a blow from a mallet. The missile was carried in a sling, attached by long lines and lying at rest in a trough under the machine; when triggered, the beam sprang upward through an arc, gaining acceleration before the missile was picked up. Consequently, high "muzzle velocity" [speed] could be achieved, especially if the missile was released at near the optimum angle of 45 degrees.

Frances Gies and Joseph Gies, *Cathedral, Forge, and Waterwheel: Technology and Invention in the Middle Ages*. New York: HarperCollins, 1994, p. 146.

perhaps more, and some catapults had a range of several hundred feet. By adjusting the point at which the missile was released, soldiers could improve their chances of hitting their intended target. A steady bombardment of heavy boulders against the wall of a castle could quickly inflict serious damage. If attackers changed the angle of flight slightly, they could send missiles into the bailey as well; this could kill unsuspecting defenders, and even if it did not hit anyone, the sight of a boulder sailing over the wall was guaranteed to terrify the people inside.

Catapults launched materials other than rocks, too. "Any large, weighty, or unpleasant object might serve,"[36] notes historian Jim

The siege of Harlech Castle in Wales (pictured) in 1294 failed largely because the attackers could not prevent the flow of supplies to the castle by sea. Supply routes on land could often be blocked, but castles built along coastlines had the added advantage of using boats for their needs.

Bradbury. Often, for example, the rotting, disease-infested corpses of animals were lobbed over the walls via trebuchet or mangonel. The main purpose was to spread infection, but even if that failed, the tactic succeeded in disgusting the castle inhabitants. Attackers also used catapults to engage in psychological warfare. As historian Alan Baker writes, "It was quite common to hurl the heads of captured soldiers over the walls."[37] Finally, even in an era of stone castles, armies occasionally set grass or hay on fire and sent it soaring into the castle bailey. Though fire had little effect on stone, it could ignite wooden buildings and other materials, causing potentially great damage.

Because catapults were large and bulky, they were not easily portable and had to be built at the castle site. Despite this drawback, they were highly valued weapons. In 1304, for instance, Edward I captured Stirling Castle in Scotland by using a huge trebuchet nicknamed Warwolf. "With one blow, Warwolf leveled a section of wall," reads one account of the action, "successfully concluding the siege."[38] On Ibiza, an island off the Spanish coast, a castle surrendered in 1114 after invaders launched just ten stones against the wall. And even when catapults could not knock down a wall altogether, they could still cause serious harm. The Tower of London was nearly captured in 1267 when an attacking army sent a barrage of boulders into its walls.

The best defense against a catapult was a thick wall, but even that could not prevent boulders from being tossed over the palisades. Neither could defenders trust that any wall, no matter how strong, would stand up to a sustained barrage. Castle defenders therefore had few options in the face of a catapult attack. Archers inside the castle walls could fire at the men building the machines or the men launching the missiles, but the distances were great, and most arrows failed to find their targets. Several medieval battles featured warring catapults, in which the defenders used their own throwing machines to try to smash the enemy's trebuchets and ballistas. According to medieval warrior and author Philip of

Novara, for instance, the forces holding Cyprus's Kyrenia Castle in 1232 hired "many good makers of engines,"[39] or catapults, to protect it from an extended attack.

Miners

Another strategy often employed by attackers was sapping or mining. In this tactic, diggers tried to tunnel their way beneath the castle walls. A temporary wall shielded the start of the tunnel from the lookouts stationed in the castle's parapets, making it impossible for the defenders to know when miners were at work or where they were heading. The purpose of the tunnels was to undermine the castle's walls and towers, weakening them by creating holes below the foundations. Though the work was taxing and uncomfortable, the miners often succeeded in their assignment. In 1231 a castle in Beirut, in what is now Lebanon, was nearly defeated in just this way. "The castle was so mined . . . it was falling in pieces,"[40] an eyewitness reported; only the arrival of reinforcements saved the day for the defenders.

Even when the tunnels failed to weaken the towers and walls directly, they were still useful; the hollow spaces below the foundations could be filled with wood and set on fire. In many cases the fire would spread through the foundation, perhaps engulfing the bailey with flames and possibly damaging the wall. This strategy was used to great effect by King Philip II of France in an assault on Château Gaillard in Normandy. A raging fire belowground combined with an unrelenting bombardment of the castle walls by trebuchets succeeded in knocking down one part of the wall altogether. "[The wall] produces a great roar as it collapses," wrote an observer. "A cloud of smoke whirls upwards in a twisting vortex . . . and the ruin belches out a great dust cloud that mushrooms out above."[41]

Mining was difficult to prevent, but several responses to it were effective. The first was to build a castle on solid rock, or rock as solid as possible; tunneling through earth was feasible, but digging through rock was not. The second was to construct a moat around the castle, preferably one filled with water. That forced diggers to tunnel under the moat, adding distance and difficulty to their task. A third solution developed through trial and error. Rectangular towers, the norm

 "A SIEGE SO HARD PRESSED"

In some medieval battles castles proved almost impenetrable, and the fighting ended quickly when the attackers realized they could not overcome the defense. In others, the opposite occurred: invaders successfully stormed the castle within days of arriving, as the castle's defenses were no match for the attackers' tactics. Sometimes, however, the two sides were more or less evenly matched. Then the result was an extended series of attacks and counterattacks that severely weakened both sides.

One good example of this kind of battle took place in 1215 during a conflict known as the First Barons' War. Rochester Castle in southeastern England was firmly under the control of a group of barons who had rebelled against England's King John. In October, however, forces loyal to the king besieged the castle. The defenders refused to surrender, so the king's army tried to damage the castle walls with trebuchets and other throwing machines. When that failed, they dug a tunnel, causing one of the castle's towers to collapse and allowing them entry to part of the castle. Even then the defenders held out; they retreated to another part of the castle and continued to fight back. Finally, seven weeks after the attack began, the barons ran out of food and surrendered. "Our age has not known a siege so hard pressed nor so strongly resisted," wrote one awed chronicler.

Quoted in Nicholas Hooper and Matthew Bennett, *The Cambridge Illustrated Atlas of Warfare: The Middle Ages, 768–1487*. Cambridge, UK: Cambridge University Press, 1996, p. 64.

in early medieval castles, turned out to be especially susceptible to mining; hollowing out space below one corner could make the whole structure tip dangerously. By replacing rectangular towers with circular ones, castle builders could eliminate this vulnerability.

Still, mining was always a possibility, and so castle defenders learned to watch for signs of activity below the foundations. Setting a pot of water in the basement of a tower was one way of detecting digging: if the water sloshed back and forth, something was probably going on beneath it. Defenders sometimes dug tunnels of their own, hoping to intercept the attackers while not disturbing the foundations any further. If they found evidence of mining, they would fill the tunnels with water or try to kill the diggers in some other way. In one case, Bradbury writes, forces in the castle "put ale and water in great cauldrons, boil[ed] it, and drop[ped] it on the miners so that 'their skin peeled off'"[42]—a response that was as effective as it was cruel.

Storming the Castle

A more direct style of attack was known as the escalade. This tactic was used mainly when the attacking forces were much more numerous than the defenders. In an escalade, attackers dashed forward to the castle walls with long ladders, leaned the ladders against the walls, and climbed up. The goal was to reach the palisades and swarm into the castle before the defenders could react. Ideally, so many attackers would reach the top that the defenders would be forced to surrender. Even if only a few made it over the wall, they could create a diversion while other soldiers attempted to enter the castle through some other means. Escalades were often carried out at night, the better to catch the defenders by surprise.

Escalades, however, were limited in their effectiveness. They were not feasible when the walls were very high or where a moat surround-

WORDS IN CONTEXT

escalade
Use of ladders to climb a castle's walls.

An invading army leans its ladders against a castle's wall in preparation for an attack. The goal was to swarm the castle from above or to create a distraction that would allow troops below to enter by other means.

ed the castle, and they were risky under any circumstances. Once alerted to the attack, defenders had many ways of thwarting an escalade. Men on the parapets waited till the invaders were halfway to the tops of the walls—and then pushed the ladders away from the stonework. Bowmen shot a barrage of arrows at the men ascending the ladders; defenders boiled water, tar, or other liquids and dumped these on the soldiers below. The attacking forces typically posted archers of their own to fire at the palisades, threatening defenders who ventured out too far. But an escalade rarely succeeded if the garrison promptly noticed the attack.

To improve their chances of getting over the walls, attackers often built massive devices called belfries or siege towers. A belfry was a wooden tower, often mounted on wheels, that rose as much as 100 feet (30 m) into the air; some may have been even taller. Belfries contained multiple platforms at different heights, with ladders connecting them. These siege towers could be rolled up to the castle walls, whereupon soldiers would storm up the ladders and onto the upper platforms. These were carefully calibrated to match the approximate height of the palisade, which would in turn allow the soldiers access to the castle.

Belfries had some of the same drawbacks as escalades. They were difficult to use if a castle was elevated well above the ground or if the castle had a moat. And because the towers were placed directly beside the castle walls, invaders were extremely vulnerable to arrows, boiling water, and other counterattacks. In particular, defenders often tried to set the siege towers on fire. Belfries also were prone to getting stuck in mud or sand as they moved forward, and they tipped over if they crossed surfaces that were not perfectly flat. "We would not employ again that device,"[43] James I of Aragon pledged grimly in 1233 after his army's elaborate and expensive siege tower became completely stuck halfway to the wall during an attack on a Spanish castle.

However, siege towers did present serious problems for castle defenders. The platforms protected the attacking soldiers as they ascended to the top, and the belfries could not be pushed away like the ladders used in an escalade. Belfries also often concealed battering rams which could be used to smash in the castle gate or weak spots along the walls. Again, castle defenses evolved to counteract these devices. In one Middle Eastern castle, for example, a military officer built a hook that could be suspended from the top of the castle wall. The hook could be raised and lowered on the end of a rope, catching hold of the battering ram and deflecting it—or better yet, upending the entire belfry. Still, a siege tower was a force to be reckoned with and helped to defeat dozens of castles throughout the medieval era.

Bribes, Tricks, and Lavatory Chutes

Over time, castle builders adapted their designs to limit the effectiveness of all these tactics and others as well. Deep moats, thick walls, round towers—each could thwart even a determined attacker. The addition of strong catapults—used by some defenders—and skilled archers could make the fortress that much more difficult to conquer. Still, no castle was invincible. A patient attacker could usually find a way to defeat any fortress, no matter how well designed. It was possible, for instance, for an attacking force to drain a moat and fill it with dirt to provide direct access to the castle walls, and many invaders did exactly that. And even the best-defended castles had their weaknesses. One French castle fell in part because a young soldier was able to enter the fortress by shinnying up a lavatory chute. As one writer puts it, the boy's dedication "was surely above and beyond the call of duty."[44]

Well-protected castles could fall through human error or greed, too. Defending armies sometimes surrendered long before they needed to, under the mistaken belief that the attacking force was larger than it was. Several castles were conquered through bribery, where guards, soldiers, or commanders admitted forces to the stronghold in exchange for money—a favorite tactic of Henry IV, a German king of the late 1000s. Finally, trickery could be highly effective. In one notable case from 1314, for example, Scottish soldiers outside Britain's Roxburgh Castle concealed themselves under cowhides one night and crawled to the walls, whereupon they threw off their disguises and mounted an escalade, taking the defenders by surprise and capturing the castle.

What with treachery, bribery, and the element of surprise, castles were never immune to conquest. Still, as attackers developed new weapons and more effective tactics, the people who built and designed castles more than kept pace. The replacement of wood with stone, double-wall constructions, deeper ditches—all of these features, and many others, were effective responses to changes in medieval warfare. As time passed, castles did become increasingly difficult to defeat, and the largest of them—notably Edward I's castles in Wales—were very nearly unconquerable by standard weapons and military tactics. Tested again and again by war, the castles of the Middle Ages evolved to meet the challenges. They are an excellent example of how architecture and building methods can change over time—and for the better.

CHAPTER FIVE

The Medieval Castle Today

The era of the castle did not last for long after the end of the Middle Ages. Since the late 1500s very few castles have been constructed—and most of those are fantasy castles in amusement parks and other entertainment venues, none of them meant to be taken as anything other than imitations of the castles of the Middle Ages. To be sure, many castles originally built in the medieval period are still standing. The care taken in their construction, especially in the later part of the era, guaranteed that some remain even after the passage of five centuries or more. However, none of them are used for defensive purposes any longer, and none have been for a good many years. Today, castles are a relic of a bygone age.

Nonetheless, even in modern times, castles still play a role in European life. The castles of the Middle Ages continue to dot the map of Europe; some are little more than ruins, but others are still in decent condition. A few remain in use as homes for the wealthy and particularly for monarchs. Windsor Castle in England, for example, is the main home of the British royal family. Others have been repurposed to serve as hotels or museums. And many medieval castles are tourist attractions, bringing in travelers eager to soak up the history and the romance of the medieval era. Recognizing

> **WORDS IN CONTEXT**
> repurposed
> *Used in a new way.*

the cultural, historical, and economic value of this heritage, European countries have increasingly taken steps to preserve the castles that remain. If all goes well, the rich history of castles will be available to people for many generations to come.

The Effect of Cannons

Though castle design changed successfully in dozens of ways over a period of many centuries, there was one innovation that castles could not adapt to. That was gunpowder. Originally developed in China, gunpowder first became known to Europeans sometime in the mid-1200s. For about one hundred years, however, it was seldom used in warfare. Difficult to manufacture and not always reliable in battle, gunpowder was generally used only as an adjunct to tried-and-true military technologies such as bows and arrows, spears, and catapults. In 1338, for instance, French forces used just three pounds (1.4 kg) of gunpowder on a raid of England.

But forward-thinking strategists recognized that gunpowder could be extremely useful in warfare. During the second half of the 1300s, as the Middle Ages were drawing to a close, Europeans worked diligently to develop better recipes for gunpowder and to find new ways of using it in battle. In particular, military leaders realized that gunpowder could be used to fire cannons, sending heavy metal balls just as far as a trebuchet could lob them—and with a good deal more power. By the end of the 1300s, cannons were widely used in warfare throughout Europe—though as Peter Purton points out, "it was by no means guaranteed that the gunpowder artillery of this date was more useful in battering medieval walls than the great stones still hurled with great destructive impact by weapons of the trebuchet type."[45]

That changed quickly, however. As gunpowder became easier to make and easier to use, cannons became more and more effective, and military leaders became increasingly interested in their capabilities. In the early 1400s, for the first time in European history, guns began to be more important in warfare than other weap-

Windsor Castle in England is the oldest and largest occupied castle in the world. It covers an area of about 13 acres (5 hectares) and is the official residence of the queen. Pictured is one of the castle's many richly decorated rooms.

ons. Cannons had become more powerful and accurate than even the strongest catapult, and they were increasingly reliable as well. Indeed, they had developed to such a point that they could fire a cannonball through all but the thickest, strongest castle walls. The growing effectiveness of cannons was clearly demonstrated for all Europe to see in the early 1450s, when the French army used the power of the huge guns to smash their way into a number of castles held by English forces.

The era of the castle was drawing to a close. Castles were simply no longer able to keep attackers away—their primary function—and so they were gradually abandoned in favor of lower, squatter fortifications with thicker walls and no room for nobles and their family. By the 1500s, write Frances Gies and Joseph Gies, the castle had been "superseded by the low-profile, thick-rampart fortress, capable of absorbing the shock of heavy cannonballs and furnishing a good platform for defensive artillery but ill adapted to service as a private residence."[46] Few military strategists considered castles worth defending, and essentially no one considered them worth constructing. The fortifications of the Middle Ages were obsolete.

Centuries of Neglect

Between the 1500s and the 1800s many castles fell into ruin. Few were destroyed outright; tearing a castle down, especially one of any significant size, would have required far more labor and expense than anyone could willingly afford. But many of the castles of the Middle Ages were more or less abandoned—and when maintenance stopped, the castles began to disintegrate. In some cases the process was aided by fire, earthquake, or other natural disaster. Quite a few Portuguese castles, for example, were badly damaged by an earthquake that ripped through the country in 1755. The Alvor Castle, among others, was almost completely destroyed by the shock waves.

Other castles crumbled in part because of the actions of people who lived nearby. During the 1600s, for example, the inhabitants of towns close to Urquhart Castle in Scotland began pulling blocks out of the structure's walls and towers. They reasoned that these materials would be quite useful in building houses for themselves—and with the castle no longer in use, there was no one

MAD KING LUDWIG AND NEUSCHWANSTEIN

Though castles went out of fashion as military installations soon after the close of the Middle Ages, some wealthy Europeans continued to build structures that were similar to castles for many years afterward. Among the most famous of these builders was a nineteenth-century German monarch named Ludwig II of Bavaria, but better known as Mad King Ludwig. Ludwig certainly had his share of peculiarities. Contemporary accounts describe him as more or less nocturnal, prone to dressing up in historic costumes—even for mundane activities—and increasingly reclusive as he aged.

In the late 1800s Ludwig ordered the construction of a medieval-style castle where he could completely withdraw from public life. The castle, called Neuschwanstein, was begun in 1869. Nestled in a gorgeous spot by the German Alps and surrounded by lakes and forests, the castle was a fantasy come true, with towers and spires mixed in with modern conveniences such as running water and central heating systems.

Ludwig died in 1886, before the castle was finished, but Neuschwanstein was close enough to completion that it was opened to the public soon afterward. It remains one of Germany's top tourist attractions, with an average of six thousand visitors a day during the summer months. Though it is by no means an authentic re-creation of a Middle Ages castle, it represents the romantic view of the medieval period common in the 1800s—and it is a remarkable structure in its own right as well.

to stop them. The result was predictable. By the early 1700s, after almost a century of this kind of treatment, the castle began to collapse. As one report of the time puts it, Urquhart Castle had become so weak that a single "Storme of Wind"[47] was sufficient to blow down a large section of the wall.

Some castles did remain in use in the years following the Middle Ages, though rarely as defensive bulwarks. Instead, they were converted to other uses. Oxford Castle in England, for example, was used as an administrative center for county government—and through most of the 1500s as a prison as well. Celje Castle in what is now Slovenia was used as offices by tax collectors. The Parador de Tortosa, a castle in Spain, became a courthouse. Several castles that had once housed entire regiments of knights and other soldiers now became warehouses where weapons, construction materials, or foods were stored. Chillon Castle, on the shores of Lake Geneva in Switzerland, became at various times a storehouse, a hospital, and an armory.

Other former castles were turned into permanent residences, usually for members of the upper classes. The larger castles often became

Once one of Scotland's largest castles, Urquhart Castle (pictured) now stands in ruins on the banks of Loch Ness. Over time, the inhabitants of nearby towns pulled blocks out of the structure's walls and towers for use in building their own houses.

palaces, with the rooms in the keep being enlarged and the outer walls left to crumble; smaller castles sometimes were turned into homes for the very rich. During the late 1500s, for example, Debno Castle in Poland was the private property of a Polish nobleman named Ferenc Wesselini, and a single family has lived at Eltz Castle in Germany for over thirty generations. Though the accommodations in these former castles could be spacious and the views exceptional, the nobles who owned these buildings were fully responsible for upkeep, which was often staggering. The result, as Frances Gies and Joseph Gies put it, was that the castles all too often "sank to the status of not very comfortable country houses."[48]

Castles and the Romantics

But even the castles that were still in use following the medieval period were often changed substantially to match their new uses. In an effort to save money, for instance, a noble family might close off entire wings of a castle, thereby allowing them to disintegrate. Similarly, the rooms of a keep might be remodeled to make them more suitable as offices. Any redecoration or rebuilding, moreover, would usually be carried out with different materials and a different sense of style from what was popular when the castle was originally built. Through the 1700s no one cared much about preserving castles as they had been built. The result was that the castles that remained from the medieval period gradually moved further and further away from their original design.

Beginning in the early 1800s, however, the gradual decay of Europe's castles—and the wholesale changes that had been made to others—began to bother some Europeans. Many of these people were associated with the Romantic movement in literature,

WORDS IN CONTEXT
heritage
The cultural and historic traditions of a people.

which emphasized themes of heritage and community and looked back to bygone eras for inspiration. These thinkers valued medieval castles for their rich history, and they longed to see castles as the

UNESCO AND THE WORLD HERITAGE SITES

Much of the effort to preserve castles throughout Europe has been led by an arm of the United Nations known as UNESCO—an acronym for United Nations Educational, Scientific and Cultural Organization. This group is charged in part with increasing appreciation for culture and history. To this end, UNESCO began forming a list of World Heritage Sites in the 1970s in an attempt to single out places of particular interest and value. Over nine hundred sites had been placed on the list by 2013. These include wildernesses, buildings, city centers, and much more.

One of UNESCO's purposes in making the list is to highlight the existence of these places and let people know of the wealth of resources on the planet. Another is to lead efforts to preserve these unique places. UNESCO cannot mandate specific preservation techniques or control what individual countries do with the sites on the list. Still, listed sites often receive needed funding for restoration from both public and private sources. The designation of one example of a particular architectural style as a heritage site, moreover, encourages similar efforts on behalf of similar structures. Without UNESCO, castle preservation would be much less robust today.

people of the Middle Ages had seen them. To them, the ruined and repurposed castles around Europe represented an insult to the spirit of the Middle Ages and the designers and laborers who had struggled to build the fortresses.

Several of the Romantics wrote poems, plays, and other works set in medieval times, many of them featuring castles. Sir Walter Scott of Great Britain wrote novels such as *Ivanhoe*, published in 1820 but set in 1194, which glorified the medieval world. And in 1803 German writer Johann Wolfgang von Goethe wrote a nostalgic poem called "The Mountain Castle," in which the narrator visits a ruined castle and imagines what it would have been like hundreds of years before. "Below once lay a cellar/With costly wines well stor'd," the poem runs. "No more for the eager squire/The draught [drink] in the passage is pour'd."[49] Works like these sparked a wider interest in all things medieval: medieval culture, medieval monarchs, and perhaps most particularly medieval castles.

By the middle of the 1800s the Romantics and other influential Europeans had begun to lobby for the restoration of castles. They urged private and public funders alike to rebuild castles that had tumbled into ruin and to reverse the changes in castles that had been redesigned over the centuries. They also appealed to patriotic sentiment to encourage government leaders to spend money on these projects, arguing that restoring castles would be an acknowledgment of a country's impressive heritage and thereby increase national pride. It helped that the 1800s were fundamentally a prosperous time throughout much of Europe; this made it possible for national leaders and private citizens to consider spending the enormous sums necessary to rebuild medieval castles.

Wartburg Castle

One of the first castles to undergo this kind of restoration was Wartburg Castle in central Germany. Wartburg was of particular historic and cultural importance. Construction on the fortress had begun in 1067, and it had been home to several generations of German princes. Later, in the early 1500s, religious reformer Martin Luther had hidden in the castle to avoid arrest by Church authorities. Over the years, the castle had been significantly altered. Under the leadership of the Grand Duke of Saxony, however, the castle was restored to what nineteenth-century officials and historians believed it had looked like years earlier. "The entire site was completely renovated," explains a website describing the changes. "The remains of the palace were raised from their ruins, the . . . wall restored, and the remainder of the buildings reconstructed."[50]

From a historical perspective the renovation of Wartburg Castle was not entirely accurate. Historians and archeologists of the mid-1800s did not know nearly as much about the castles of the Middle

Ages as their counterparts do today. As a result, they were forced to make some suppositions about what Wartburg looked like, and some of what they believed turned out to be wrong. In part this was due to wishful thinking; as the UNESCO website puts it, "The large parts played by assumptions in the reconstruction have rather more to do with the romantic imagination than with historical reality."[51] Still, even if the execution of the restoration left something to be desired, the motives of those behind the project were solid. Wartburg marked the beginning of a new way of thinking about castles—and of thinking about history in general.

Preservation and Restoration

Through the rest of the 1800s and into the 1900s, European governments and private organizations gradually became more and more interested in preserving—and restoring—their castles. The process was interrupted for a time in the early- to-mid-1900s due to two world wars and a devastating economic depression. Indeed, World War II set the cause back considerably, as dozens of castles throughout Europe sustained serious harm in bombing raids and other attacks. Some of these structures had already been substantially rebuilt to restore their original grandeur. That was the case with Malbork Castle in Poland, for example, which had been widely recognized as an outstanding example of restoration before World War II but was badly damaged in the closing days of the war.

Following World War II, however, the pace of restorations increased, and preservation of medieval castles soon became popular throughout most of Europe. Preservation efforts were given a particular boost in the 1970s, when the United Nations (UN) began identifying important cultural, historic, and natural sites around the globe. These were designated as World Heritage Sites, and the UN urged that they be preserved in their original condition as much as was practicable. Today, World Heritage Sites include the Welsh castles built by England's King Edward I, the Tower of London, a set of medieval fortifications in Switzerland known as the Three Castles of Bellinzona, and many more.

Most European nations have compiled similar lists of their own, and many of these lists likewise include castles. Indeed, quite a few countries have established government agencies or nonprofit organizations charged specifically with caring for the nation's castles. In the United Kingdom, for instance, the National Trust is responsible for maintaining and preserving several hundred historic buildings, including some of the country's remaining medieval castles. The goal is to make these structures available to anyone who wants to see them. As the organization describes its mission, "We open them up for ever, for everyone."[52]

But preservation takes a great deal of money, and the need for funds outstrips the available supply. As a result, many medieval castles are in such an advanced state of disrepair that very little can save them at this point. These buildings have gaping holes in their roofs and grass growing in ornamental ponds. Some have been closed off entirely for fear that whole sections of the walls will collapse onto unsuspecting visitors. A German historic preservation agency categorizes over one hundred German castles as "without prospects"[53]—almost impossible to repair without enormous infusions of cash. Many castles, and not just in Germany, have essentially no chance of surviving much longer.

Repurposing Castles

Overall, however, efforts to preserve castles have been quite successful. In particular, many medieval castles are often billed as tourist attractions—a use very much in keeping with their status as cultural and historic treasures. Many of these structures have become extremely popular destinations. Heidelberg Castle in Germany, for example, receives about 3 million visitors every year. Bran Castle in Romania has successfully marketed itself as the home of

Bran Castle in Romania (pictured) has successfully marketed itself as the home of the legendary Count Dracula. It is the most-visited site in the country.

the legendary Count Dracula; today, it is the most-visited site in the country. Windsor Castle is still the home of Britain's royal family, but parts of the complex are open to tourists, and hundreds of thousands of visitors tour these parts each year.

Other castles dating from the Middle Ages have been converted into commercial establishments. Quite a few medieval castles now serve as hotels, for example. One of the most famous of these is the Castell d'Empordà in Spain. Built originally during the 1300s, this castle became a thirty-seven-room hotel in 1999. The advertising for the hotel leans heavily on the building's historical value. "Where else can you stay in a luxurious room in an eight hundred year old castle?"[54] one website asks. And while many of the castles that are now hotels were transformed in the last two or three decades, some were converted earlier. Ashford Castle in Ireland, for example, was turned into a hotel in the 1940s.

Some castles of the Middle Ages have become museums or galleries. In Halle, Germany, for example, the Moritzburg Museum houses a collection of fine art in what was once a castle from the late Middle Ages. This building is particularly interesting because it had fallen into a state of acute disrepair, including losing its entire roof over the centuries. Rather than rebuilding the castle in its original style, the designers opted for a much more modern feel. According to many observers, the combination of old and new is quite successful. As one travel blog puts it, the castle now includes "a second-floor extension of modern steel, glass, and stark white plaster, contrasting beautifully with the 15th century stonework."[55]

The recycled castles of the twenty-first century may serve other purposes as well. Some are part of college campuses. University College in England, for example, owns and uses the former Durham Castle. Originally built in the eleventh century, this structure is now a dormitory and a dining hall. Others are used by government agencies. In Bergen, Norway, the Sverresborg—a large and historic castle dating from the 1180s—houses military offices today, an appropriate use for a building that once protected Norwegian lands. Still others are restaurants, apartment buildings, or even wedding venues; as one website that promotes castles for weddings tells potential customers, "It's the day that a bride wants to feel like a princess and what better way to make that happen than to celebrate your wedding in a castle?"[56]

The variety of ways that castles are used today would certainly surprise the medieval Europeans who designed and built the original castles. It is difficult to know what Master James of St. George would have made of castles-turned-hotels, say, or what Edward I would have thought of selling tickets for the four o'clock tour of one of the Welsh castles he bankrolled. In another way, however, the use of castles in modern times is entirely in keeping with the history of the medieval castle. Throughout the Middle Ages, after all, castles evolved to suit the needs of the people who owned them. The simple motte and bailey construction of the 800s gave way to more complex building methods as weapons and military strategies developed; the short log walls of early medieval castles became tall, thick masonry barriers as the occasion demanded. In this sense, the story of castles through time is the story of constant reinvention. Viewed in this light, using castles as restaurants, dormitories, and museums is simply a response to the needs of a new era—and as a result, it makes perfect sense.

WORDS IN CONTEXT

masonry
Made of stone.

SOURCE NOTES

Chapter One: Beginnings and Influences

1. Elspeth Whitney, *Medieval Science and Technology*. Westport, CT: Greenwood, 2004, p. 113.
2. Frances Gies and Joseph Gies, *Cathedral, Forge, and Waterwheel: Technology and Invention in the Middle Ages*. New York: Harper-Collins, 1994, p. 141.
3. Quoted in Peter Purton, *A History of the Late Medieval Siege: 1200–1500*. Woodbridge, UK: Boydell and Brewer, 2010, p. 11.
4. Jean-Denis Lepage, *Castles and Fortified Cities of Medieval Europe: An Illustrated History*. Jefferson, NC: McFarland, 2002, p. 9.
5. Maurice Keen, *Medieval Warfare: A History*. Oxford, UK: Oxford University Press, 1999, pp. 2–3.
6. Quoted in Anna Ritchie, "Loot and Land," BBC History, February 17, 2011. www.bbc.co.uk.
7. Lepage, *Castles and Fortified Cities of Medieval Europe*, p. 28.
8. Quoted in Kelly DeVries and Robert Douglas, *Medieval Military Technology*. Toronto, ON: University of Toronto Press, 2012, p. 213.
9. Quoted in Ella S. Armitage, *The Early Norman Castles of the British Isles*. London: John Murray, 1912, p. 148.
10. Quoted in Armitage, *The Early Norman Castles of the British Isles*, p. 147.
11. Quoted in DeVries and Douglas, *Medieval Military Technology*, p. 213.

Chapter Two: Gates, Rooms, and Towers

12. R. Allen Brown, *Castles from the Air*. Cambridge, UK: Cambridge University Press, 1989, p. 47.
13. Ramon Muntaner, *The Catalan Expedition to the East: From the Chronicle of Ramon Muntaner*, trans. Robert D. Hughes. Woodbridge, UK: Tamesis, 2006, p. 93.

14. J.E. Kaufmann, H. W. Kaufmann, and Robert M. Jurga, *The Medieval Fortress*. Cambridge, MA: Da Capo, 2004, p. 31.

15. Castles and Manor Houses Around the World, "Castle Architecture." www.castlesandmanorhouses.com.

16. Lepage, *Castles and Fortified Cities of Medieval Europe*, p. 121.

17. Gies and Gies, *Cathedral, Forge, and Waterwheel*, p. 140.

18. Quoted in Armitage, *The Early Norman Castles of the British Isles*, pp. 147–148.

19. Quoted in Armitage, *The Early Norman Castles of the British Isles*, p. 89.

20. Marian Moffett, Michael W. Fazio, and Lawrence Wodehouse, *A World History of Architecture*. London: Laurence King, 2003.

21. Jeffrey Singman, *Daily Life in Medieval Europe*. Westport, CT: Greenwood, 1999, p. 119.

22. Barbara Tuchman, *A Distant Mirror*. New York: Knopf, 1978, p. 235.

Chapter Three: Constructing a Castle

23. Tuchman, *A Distant Mirror*, p. 5.

24. R.A. Stalley, *Early Medieval Architecture*. Oxford, UK: Oxford University Press, 1999, p. 103.

25. Nigel Jones, *Tower*. London: Hutchinson, 2012, p. 7.

26. Arnold Taylor, "The Beaumaris Castle Building Account of 1295–1298," in John R. Kenyon and Richard Avent, eds., *Castles in Wales and the Marches: Essays in Honour of D.J. Catheart King*. Cardiff, UK: University of Wales Press, p. 125.

27. Quoted in Gies and Gies, *Cathedral, Forge, and Waterwheel*, p. 192.

28. Quoted in Tom McNeill, *English Heritage Book of Castles*. London: B.T. Batsford/English Heritage, 1992, p. 43.

29. Quoted in McNeill, *English Heritage Book of Castles*, p. 43.

30. Quoted in A.J. Taylor, *The Welsh Castles of England*. London: Hambledon, 2009, p. 15.

31. Gies and Gies, *Cathedral, Forge, and Waterwheel*, p. 144.

Chapter Four: Castles and Warfare

32. Jean Froissart, *Stories from Froissart*, trans. Henry Newbolt. New York: Macmillan, 1899, p. 34.

33. Richard Erdoes, *A.D. 1000: Living on the Brink of Apocalypse*. Berkeley, CA: Seastone, 1998, p. 14.

34. Edward Augustus Freeman, *The Reign of William Rufus and the Accession of Henry the First*. Oxford, UK: Oxford University Press, 1882.

35. Quoted in Alan Baker, *The Knight*. New York: Wiley, 2003, p. 101.

36. Jim Bradbury, *The Medieval Siege*. Woodbridge, UK: Boydell and Brewer, 1992, p. 257.

37. Baker, *The Knight*, p. 89.

38. Quoted in PBS, "Secrets of Lost Empires: The Medieval Siege," *NOVA*, February 1, 2000. www.pbs.org.

39. Quoted in Purton, *A History of the Late Medieval Siege*, p. 24.

40. Quoted in Purton, *A History of the Late Medieval Siege*, p. 23.

41. Quoted in Baker, *The Knight*, p. 104.

42. Bradbury, *The Medieval Siege*, p. 42.

43. Quoted in Purton, *A History of the Late Medieval Siege*, p. 48.

44. Baker, *The Knight*, p. 104.

Chapter Five: The Medieval Castle Today

45. Purton, *A History of the Late Medieval Siege*, p. 402.

46. Gies and Gies, *Cathedral, Forge, and Waterwheel*, p. 250.

47. About Scotland, "Castle Urquhart." www.aboutscotland.com.

48. Gies and Gies, *Cathedral, Forge, and Waterwheel*, p. 250.

49. Johann Wolfgang von Goethe, *The Poems of Goethe*, trans. Edgar Alfred Bowring. London: John W. Parker, 1853, p. 91.

50. UNESCO, "Wartburg Castle." http://whc.unesco.org.

51. UNESCO, "Wartburg Castle," http://whc.unesco.org.

52. National Trust, "What We Do." www.nationaltrust.org.uk.

53. Matthias Schulz, "Castles Without Kings: Saving the Castles of the German Hinterland," *Der Spiegel*, June 4, 2012. www.spiegel.de.

54. Inns of Spain, "Castell d'Emporda." www.innsofspain.com.

55. Webecoist, "Converted Castles." http://webecoist.momtastic.com.

56. Celtic Castles, "VIP Wedding Planner. www.vipweddingplanner.com.

FACTS ABOUT MEDIEVAL CASTLES

Height

- Usual height for the motte of a large motte and bailey: 30 feet (9 m).
- Height of the walls of Framlingham Castle in England: 40 feet (12 m).
- Height of the keep at Dover Castle in England: 80 feet (24 m).
- Height of the tallest tower at Warwick Castle in England: 128 feet (39 m).
- Number of steps in the staircase leading to the top tower of the Alcázar de Segovia in Spain: 152.

Thickness and Length

- Average thickness of a stone castle wall: 7 feet (2 m).
- Thickness of the walls at Chepstow Castle in Wales: 20 feet (6 m).
- Thickness of some of the walls at Borl Castle in Croatia: 40 feet (12 m).
- Approximate length of the wall at Conwy Castle in Wales: 1,400 yards (1,280 m).

Area

- Area covered by the bailey in a standard motte and bailey: 3 acres (1 ha).
- Area covered by Malbork Castle in Poland: 5 square miles (13 square km).
- Approximate dimensions of the largest keeps: 100 feet by 100 feet (30.5 m by 30.5 m).
- Volume of stone contained in the keep of the Château de Langeais in France: 1,556 cubic yards (1,190 cubic m).

Cost and Labor

- Length of time needed to build Château Gaillard in France: 1 year.
- Usual length of a construction season for castle builders: 8 months.
- Height of a stone wall that laborers could build in a single construction season: 10 feet (3 m).
- Usual length of time necessary to build a large stone castle: 10 years.
- Approximate size of the labor force needed to build a castle in Wales in the late 1200s: 3,000 workers.
- Minimum cost to England's King Edward I of building five castles in Wales in the late 1200s: £50,000 ($500 million in today's US dollars).

Frequency

- Number of castles held by the king of England in 1214: 93.
- Estimated number of castles and castle sites still visible in England: 1,500.
- Estimated number of castles constructed in Western Europe during the Middle Ages: 75,000.

FOR FURTHER RESEARCH

Books

Christopher Chant, *Castles*. Edison, NJ: Chartwell, 2009.

Kelly DeVries and Robert Douglas, *Medieval Military Technology*. Toronto, ON: University of Toronto Press, 2012.

Christopher Gravett, *English Castles 1200–1300*. Oxford, UK: Osprey, 2009.

Philip Steele, *Knights and Castles*. New York: Kingfisher, 2008.

Charles Stephenson, ed., *Castles: A Global History of Fortified Structures*. New York: St. Martin's Griffin, 2011.

World Book, ed., *The Age of Knights and Castles*. Chicago: World Book, 2011.

Websites

Castles of Britain (www.castles-of-britain.com/links.htm). This site provides links to the official sites of many British castles and a few elsewhere as well.

UNESCO World Heritage Centre, "World Heritage List" (http://whc.unesco.org/en/list). This page lists all the UNESCO World Heritage Sites selected to date. There are links to information and historical background on each site, including several important castles.

Warwick Castle, Virtual Tour (www.sphericalimages.com/warwick castle). This site allows visitors to experience Warwick Castle in England virtually.

Windsor Castle (www.royal.gov.uk/TheRoyalResidences/Windsor Castle/VirtualRooms/Overview.aspx). This site, which is the official website of the British Monarchy, provides information on Windsor Castle in England, including a virtual tour of some of the rooms.

INDEX

PICTURE CREDITS

Cover: Thinkstock Images

Maury Aaseng: 31, 50

AP Images: 71

© Bettmann/Corbis: 21

© Marco Cristofori/Corbis: 80

© Eurasia Press/Photononstop/Corbis: 60

© Walter Bibikow/JAI/Corbis: 46

© Michael Nicholson/Corbis: 38, 65

© Alfredo Dagli Orti/The Art Archive/Corbis: 43

© Roy Rainford/Robert Harding World Imagery/Corbis: 29

Thinkstock Images: 6, 7, 10, 23, 74

© Jürgen Wackenhut/imagebroker/Corbis: 17

Fol.261v Siege of the Chateau de Chinon, from the Grandes
Chroniques de France, 1375-79 (vellum), French School, (14th
century)/Bibliotheque Municipale, Castres, France/Giraudon/
The Bridgeman Art Library: 56

ABOUT THE AUTHOR

Stephen Currie has written dozens of books, including *The Black Death* and *The Renaissance* for ReferencePoint Press. He has also published educational materials and has taught at levels ranging from kindergarten to college. He lives with his family in New York State.